SILVER WIRE FUSING

JEWELRY STUDIO

SILVER WIRE FUSING

Liz Jones

INTERWEAVE PRESS
interweavebooks.com

Text © 2008 Liz Jones
Photography and Illustrations © 2008 Interweave Press LLC
All rights reserved.

INTERWEAVE PRESS
interweavebooks.com
201 East Fourth Street
Loveland, CO 80537-5655 USA
interweavebooks.com

Printed in China by Asia Pacific Offset.

Library of Congress Cataloging-in-Publication Data

Jones, Liz, 1980-
  Jewelry workshop : silver wire fusing / Liz Jones.
     p. cm.
  Includes index.
  ISBN-13: 978-1-59668-066-1 (pbk.)
  1. Jewelry making. 2. Wire craft. 3. Silver jewelry. I. Title.
  TT212.J67 2008
  745.594'2--dc22
                     2007029451

10 9 8 7 6 5 4 3 2 1

ACKNOWLEDGMENTS

Working on this book has been a fun and rewarding process. In the course of my work, I have been blessed with help from many people. Thanks to everyone who helped make this possible! First of all, everyone at Interweave Press for giving me the opportunity to work on such a great project. Special thanks to Rebecca Campbell for being so helpful with all of my neurotic tendencies. Secondly, Jennifer Worick, my friend and editor, for pushing me to do this project and holding my hand through difficult tasks. Thanks to everyone at Fusion Beads for being so supportive, both with my book project and also my ongoing jewelry education.

On a more personal note, I would not be able to do anything in life without the love and support of my family—my mom, Kathleen, for always believing in me and encouraging my creative talents; my brother Dan, for being a good influence and always having rational advice; and my kid sister Kate, for always letting me call her at 2:00 in the morning when I am frustrated and in need of a sympathetic ear. Then there's my best friend Joellyn, my roommate Jenna, Harold Gilbert, Jacob Livingston, Kriss Silva, Barb Switzer, Lisa Niven Kelly, Colin Mahler, Jennie Stephens, Nora Olsen, all of my students for loving my classes, Joyce Griffiths from Byzantium for beginning my bead obsession, Roxanne McGovern, Matt Hasemeier, Claire Leach, Crystal Joy, Dennis Dulle, Sarah Felter, Sara Bauer, Ginger Seiple, Jamie Hogsett, Aunt Susie and all of my Washington family, and last, but definitely not least, my dog, Stoli. All of these people (and my pooch) are like family (or maybe they are actual family), and I could not function without them. Thanks, guys!

INTRODUCTION: Welcome to the Jewelry Studio!

Welcome to the Jewelry Studio!

Are you ready to take your jewelry design to a completely new level? Silver fusing is just the ticket. It's a no-muss, no-fuss version of silversmithing that anybody can learn and enjoy. The chief difference between traditional silversmithing and fusing is the use of fine silver instead of sterling silver. Fine silver is pure silver, whereas sterling is 92.5 percent silver and 7.5 percent other metal, usually copper or nickel. Because it is pure silver, fine silver has a lower melting point and requires less work to finish after it is heated. When sterling is heated, the other metals oxidize on the surface, creating "fire scale" and causing the metal to look black, which requires additional steps to remove and polish. When fine silver is heated, this blackening does not happen, making silver fusing a quick and easy technique you will return to again and again to create unbelievable silver jewelry. No matter your skill level, you will soon embrace this technique, creating one or many of the projects showcased in the following chapters, before designing your own unique creations.

I've always been a wireworker, and when I learned how to fuse, it was love at first torch. Since mastering the basics, I've frankly become obsessed. I constantly play with my torch—safely, of course—looking for new designs and techniques and pushing the boundaries of what I know is tried and true.

Luckily, I am not afraid to fail or have something turn out different than I imagined. In the process, I have discovered new possibilities for fusing that I'm excited to share. I am thrilled when students return to share their newest designs with me, because they invariably come up with something completely different and uniquely theirs. That's the beauty of fusing. Whether you are eager to learn new ways to make gifts and jewelry for yourself or whether you want to take your jewelry business to a new level, fusing is a terrific technique to incorporate into your bag of tricks.

The first few chapters will orient you to the tools needed for fusing and then explore the basic skills you will need. Along the way, I will share professional tips and tricks to make your fusing experience fun, safe, and successful. Once you've mastered the basics, I will help you to grow beyond your fusing fundamentals and create beautiful, accomplished, one-of-a-kind designs.

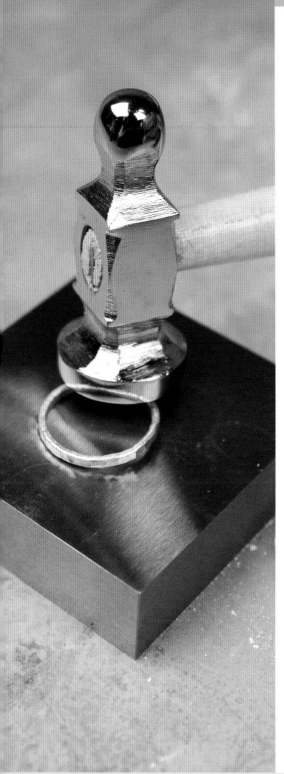

CHAPTER ONE

Tools and Materials

This chapter will introduce crafters to the various tools and materials necessary to set up a work space for fusing. Learning what tools you need and how to use them properly will put you one step closer to crafting dazzling jewelry.

THE ESSENTIAL MATERIALS

1 **Butane microtorch:** This is a small handheld butane microtorch. While it is possible to use a larger torch to fuse, this small but mighty torch will keep you happily fusing for a long time.

2 **Butane:** It's important to use good quality butane to maintain your torch. Triple- or quadruple-refined butane will be a cleaner burning fuel than regular butane, and it will be less likely to clog your torch. For long-term maintenance and optimal performance, fill your torch with a high-quality fuel.

3 **Flush cutters:** The right cutters make all the difference (see opposite page).

A Cut Above
(Liz's Musings on Cutters)

Finding a pair of flush wire cutters that can do the job right is not an easy task. I have sampled several different brands and styles of cutters in search of the perfect flush cut. Because the edges of the ring you are fusing need to be in full contact with each other, your cut needs to be as flush as possible. My favorite cutter is the Tronex razor flush wire cutters (#7223 with the ergonomic grip). This, in my opinion, is the Cadillac of cutters. The tips of these cutters are very fine, which is a great feature for wire wrapping and many different types of beading. I use my Tronex cutters on all gauges of fine silver from 14 to 30 gauge.

The only small problem with Tronex cutters is cutting heavy gauges. The reason these are *razor* flush cutters is that just below the box joint there is a little screw that prevents the two jaws of the cutter from overlapping, making the most flush cut possible. There is not enough pressure to cut through heavy gauges of fine silver in one try. I recommend using either Lindstrom cutters or a very heavy-duty pair of cutters for heavy gauges of fine silver. The only other downside to the Tronex cutters is they are not well-suited to cut heavier gauges of sterling silver. Because of the fine tips of these cutters, I do not recommend you cut anything thicker than 20 gauge in sterling silver, or you could break the tips of your cutters.

Horse Cutters

Tronex Flush Wire Cutters

Lindstrom Flush Wire Cutters

Tronex Razor Flush Wire Cutters

3

SAFETY FIRST:

When selecting a space for your fusing workstation, there are a few important things to consider. First, ventilation is extremely important. When butane burns, it produces carbon dioxide, which, in large quantities, can become hazardous. Having a window near your workstation that can be opened to provide fresh air is essential.

Make sure you do not have a fan blowing on your work space; it will blow your flame around, not allowing enough concentrated heat for fusing. If you are planning on setting up your work space on a table you use regularly, make sure you clear the surface so there are no fire hazards. Having a fire extinguisher on hand whenever you are working with an open flame is highly recommended.

I think the most important part to staying safe and injury free when you are working with an open flame is to pay attention to what you are doing. Being aware of your surroundings and where you are aiming your flame will help you have a safe, happy fusing experience.

GOOD TO KNOW:

Loose Clothing, Long Hair

Whenever you are working with an open flame, make sure you are dressed for it. Loose clothing such as scarves, big jackets, or a feather boa are not the best clothes to wear while fusing. Make sure you are wearing clothes that will not accidentally graze the flame and catch on fire. While on the subject of fire hazards, long hair should also be pulled back into a ponytail for obvious reasons (note that my hair is *medium* length in the photo at right, not long).

Protect Your Most Valuable Asset—Your Eyes

Although there will be nothing sputtering or sparking during the fusing process, whenever you are doing wirework or working with an open flame it is a good idea to protect your best tool—your eyes! Wearing tinted safety goggles will not only protect your eyes, it will also help you see the flame better. Fusing in a lower-light setting is helpful for seeing exactly how close the metal is to fusing.

Hot Spots

Not only will the firebrick get extremely hot, all of the metal components on the front of the torch get very hot and stay very hot for quite a while after the torch is turned off. Never touch a hot torch or hot firebrick surface, because it hurts!

 GOOD TO KNOW:

Firebrick on stainless-steel sheet work surface

Why Can't I Use My Favorite Pliers?

When you are selecting a pair of pliers to use for picking up your hot metal and performing other various tasks while fusing, it's a good idea to use an old, inexpensive pair of pliers. When you use the pliers in the heat of the torch, it actually anneals the metal and makes the pliers very soft. If you were then to take these pliers and try to use them for regular beading tasks, the tips would end up just being bent, and the pliers would no longer be usable.

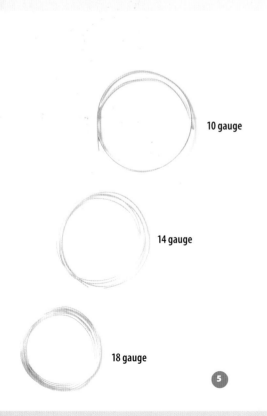

10 gauge

14 gauge

18 gauge

4 **Firebrick:** This will actually be your work surface once you start fusing. The thermal brick retains heat, which allows the metal to be heated evenly on all sides. Because it retains heat, the brick will stay hot after the torch is no longer pointed at it. The heat from the brick will actually transfer to any new metal placed on it, making the metal very hot. Pick up or move any metal on the brick using your pliers, not your fingers. And don't touch the heated area of the firebrick; if you have to reposition it, move it by touching the sides, well away from the hot surface.

5 **Fine silver** (10, 14, and, 18 gauge pictured): Fusing can only be accomplished with pure metal. Fine silver is actually 99.9 percent pure silver, verses sterling, which is 92.5 percent silver and 7.5 percent of another metal. Because it is pure metal, it has a lower melting point and requires less cleanup after it is heated. When sterling silver is heated, because of the impurities, a black "fire scale" is created on the surface. Additional steps are required to remove this. When you are working with fine silver, there is no fire scale to be removed after the metal is heated.

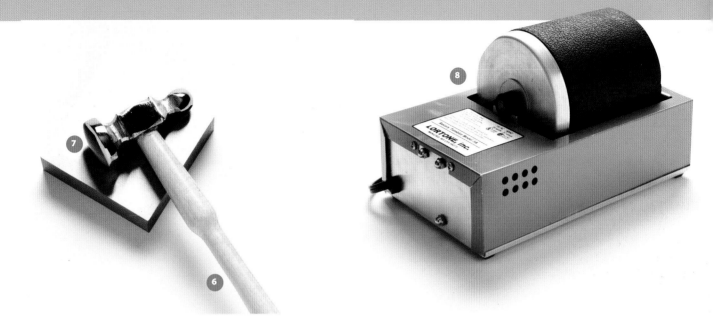

6   **Chasing hammer:** This small jewelry hammer is handy for flattening and texturing metal.

7   **Bench block** (pictured with chasing hammer): This stainless-steel block serves as a perfect surface to hammer metal on. To maintain your bench block, be careful not to hit the block with the ball end of the hammer, or it will leave small dents in your block that will show up in your metal.

8   **Tumbler:** When fine silver is heated, it is left with what looks like a brushed or matte finish. The only way to bring the metal back to a professional high shine is to tumble it. Fine silver is also a very soft metal. When it is heated, it becomes even softer. In order to make durable jewelry, it is important to strengthen the metal before it is worn. Using your tumbler is a quick, easy way to make sure your jewelry is both beautiful and strong.

9   **Stainless-steel shot:** Stainless-steel jewelry shot is actually three different-shaped shots that are designed to harden, deburr, and polish silver.

Repurposing the Sharpie

Pictured here are a few of my favorite mandrels. The ring mandrel is necessary when you are making rings for your fingers. The small-tiered mandrels also come in very handy because there are multiple sizes of mandrels on each one. But mandrels don't have to be fancy to be effective. I like repurposing household items to function as mandrels. Sharpies, pens, nail polish bottles, knitting needles—any round object can function as a mandrel. Instead of going to the hardware store and investing in a set of mandrels (I inevitably lose the one I really need), try finding items around your house that can act as makeshift mandrels. Remember that all mandrels either have to be straight or tapered so once you wrap your wire around them, you can slide the wire off. If your wire is stuck, you will not be able to cut it. Also take into account the material of your new mandrel. If it is wood or bamboo, be careful how tightly you wrap your wire around the mandrel because these materials compress with pressure. If that happens, your wire will be stuck!

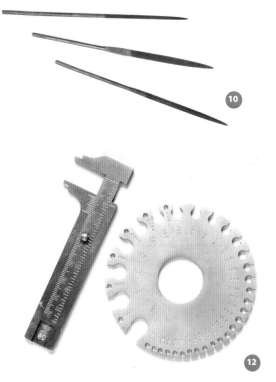

10 **Small metal jewelry files:** These are used to file down any sharp points on your metal before it is tumbled.

11 **Mandrels** (see sidebar above): Mandrels are used to shape wire into different-size rings, and they can be anything found in your house, such as a Sharpie.

12 **Calipers/brass measuring gauge:** When you are hunting for your perfect mandrel, having a pair of calipers will come in handy to measure your mandrels. Also pictured is a wire gauge, so you can determine what gauge your wire is, in case different gauge wires get jumbled together.

13 **Metal hole punch:** With two different sizes of bits, this metal hole punch is strong enough to punch holes in flattened metal.

14 **Steel wool:** Steel wool removes excess patina from metal.

15 **Metal stamps:** With a hammer and alphabet stamps, you can stamp words on flattened metal.

16 **Polishing cloth:** A polishing cloth is a quick way to buff and shine your silver jewelry.

SETTING UP YOUR WORK SPACE

You'll need all of the following items before you can start fusing:

Quenching Bowl

Firebrick

Butane Torch

Stainless-steel Sheet

- **Quenching bowl:** After you have fused your metal, using your hot-pliers, pick it up and throw it in the quenching bowl. The cold water will instantly bring the metal down to a temperature where it can be handled.

- **Firebrick:** Your work surface while fusing, firebricks retain heat, allowing metal to be heated evenly on all sides.

- **Hot-pliers:** An old, inexpensive pair of pliers used to pick up hot metal.

- **Safety glasses:** Your eyes are your most valuable asset. Wearing tinted safety glasses has a two-fold benefit—it will protect your eyes and allow you to see the flame better.

- **Stainless-steel sheet:** Protect your surfaces by working over a stainless-steel sheet, which you can find at most hardware stores.

- **Butane torch:** A small butane torch is all you need to make fabulous jewelry. Using a triple- or quadruple-refined butane will help you maintain your torch.

Safety Glasses

Hot-pliers

CHAPTER TWO

Fusing Fundamentals

Now that you know what a torch is, not to mention the other tools used in fusing, let's get going! While it is necessary to know how to care for and use your torch, mastering the cutting technique is the hardest part of the fusing process. This chapter covers the fundamentals you'll need to fuse successfully. All of the techniques in this chapter will expand your knowledge and give you the ability to create exceptional jewelry in the comfort of your home. In the words of my childhood piano teacher, practice makes perfect! Don't expect to make perfect rings the first few times; it definitely takes a little patience and practice to master your torch. But don't get discouraged, because in no time at all you will be a fusing genius.

When preparing your rings for your fused project, keep in mind that nobody is perfect. When you are first getting used to working with your torch, it is very easy to overheat rings, causing them to pull apart or just look ugly. It's a good idea to have a little extra wire on hand in case you need to make a replacement ring. Listed in all of the projects are the wire gauges and mandrel sizes needed to create the pieces as they are pictured.

WIELDING YOUR TORCH

When you are ready to fill up your torch, take a field trip outside. Whenever you are working with a compressed gas, it is an excellent idea to work in a well-ventilated area . . . like the outdoors! You don't have to travel far. Just walking outside your front door will do just fine.

FILLING YOUR TORCH

Gently shake the can of butane a few times. Turn the can upside down and line the tip of the can up with the gas intake on the bottom of your torch. Be careful to hold the butane straight up and down (left), or you can actually force oxygen down into your torch, the opposite of what we are trying to do. Press down with your can of butane with firm pressure. A completely empty torch should take between 5 and 10 seconds to

Correct   **Incorrect**

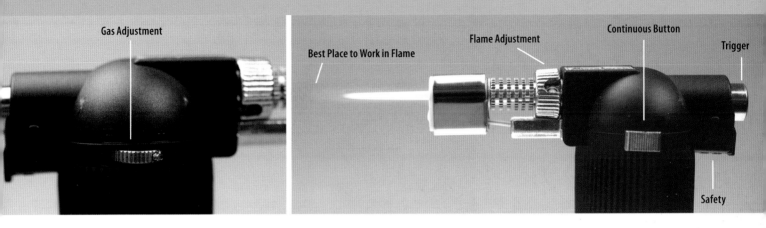

Gas Adjustment

Best Place to Work in Flame

Flame Adjustment

Continuous Button

Trigger

Safety

fill, depending on the type of torch you are using. The torch is full when butane starts to sputter back out. When this happens, stop filling your torch. Place your torch upright and leave it alone for at least 5 minutes. The gas in your torch needs a chance to settle, so it is very important to wait. Never fill a hot torch; it needs to cool before you fill it with butane.

Sometimes your torch will get clogged during the course of normal use. When your torch becomes clogged, you will notice the flame is no longer constant; instead, it will flutter or sputter. The good news? Cleaning your torch is relatively easy—all you need is a can of compressed air. Blow the compressed air gently into the tip of the torch (never stick the straw inside the torch because this can damage it) and then through the air adjustment. This should remove any clogs.

LIGHTING YOUR TORCH
Pull down on the safety until it clicks. Press and hold the trigger using your right thumb. Press and hold the "continuous" button using your left hand. Release the trigger and then take your finger off the "continuous" button. The torch should stay lit. To turn off the torch, press and release the trigger.

TOOLS AND EQUIPMENT

Tronex razor flush wire cutters

Stainless-steel work surface

Hot-pliers

Butane microtorch

Quenching bowl

Chain-nose pliers

YOU'LL NEED:

24" (61 cm) of 24-gauge fine silver wire

Need to Know

Wielding your torch (page 20)

PRACTICE: Ball Head Pins

One of the most daunting things about learning to work with metal is getting to know and love your torch. I assure you, there is nothing to fear from your torch. In fact, your torch will be your new best friend almost immediately. This first exercise will help you warm up to your torch. Your very first project (Cha Cha Earrings, page 34) will incorporate the first two techniques, so you won't waste time or wire while learning. So go ahead—don't be afraid—light up your torch!

Step 1: Cut ten 2" (5 cm) lengths of 24-gauge wire.

Step 2: With your hot-pliers, grab one end of 1 piece of wire. Hold the wire vertically in front of your torch, just past the bright blue cone. The hot-pliers should be gripping the wire at the top end, and the bottom end of the wire should be dropped down in front of the flame.

Step 3: Heat the tip of the wire until the tip starts to ball up **(Figure 1)**.

Step 4: When the desired size of ball is reached, drop the hot wire into the quenching bowl. This will immediately cool the wire to a temperature you can touch with your hands. Pull this out of the water with your hands and not your pliers. Your fingers won't rust, but the box joint of your pliers will!

TIP: Here's a trick to work-harden your head pins.

Hold your head pin by the end without the ball in your chain-nose pliers **(Figure 2)**. Grab the other balled end with your thumb and index finger and twist the ball you've just made. Twist 1½ to 2 times until the ball is hardened. Be careful not to twist the ball too many times, or it will fall off the wire.

PRACTICE: Making the Cut

The largest difference between fusing and traditional silversmithing is that there's no solder needed for fusing. Because there is no solder, the connection between the two sides of the ring must be completely flush, that is, perfectly connected and lined up with each other. If there is not direct contact between the two sides of the ring, it is likely that the wire will pull away from itself and not fuse. This becomes very expensive, as it will ruin the ring you were trying to create. Not only are the cutters important, but using them correctly is also very important. If you are not getting a perfectly flat flush cut, you will not have a very high success rate with your fusing. Read on to learn how to wield those cutters and fuse a ring, the basic component that all other techniques and variations are built upon.

Step 1: Hold the mandrel in your nondominant hand. Place the wire on the side of the mandrel facing you. Leave a 2–3" (5–7.6 cm) tail below the mandrel. If you do not leave this tail, you will be left with a very short, sharp piece of wire to hold on to while you are wrapping your coil . . . and this hurts **(Figure 1)**!

Step 2: Grab the top end of the wire and pull down and around the mandrel, laying down a neat and tidy coil **(Figure 2)**.

TOOLS AND EQUIPMENT

20 mm mandrel

Tronex razor flush wire cutters

2 pairs chain-nose pliers

YOU'LL NEED:

12" (30.5 cm) of 14-gauge fine silver wire

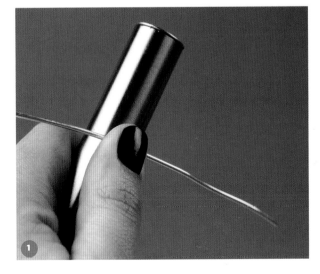

Step 3: Push the tail around the mandrel so you do not waste wire **(Figure 3)**.

Step 4: At the end of the coil, the tail that could not be pushed completely flat is still a straight piece of wire. We need to trim this off so we are left with a fully curved circle. With the flat side of the cutters facing away from the tail, cut where the curve of the circle begins **(Figure 4)**.

Step 5: Flip the cutters over, line up the tips on the next coil, exactly where you just cut the first side without recutting the first cut. Cut **(Figures 5 and 6)**!

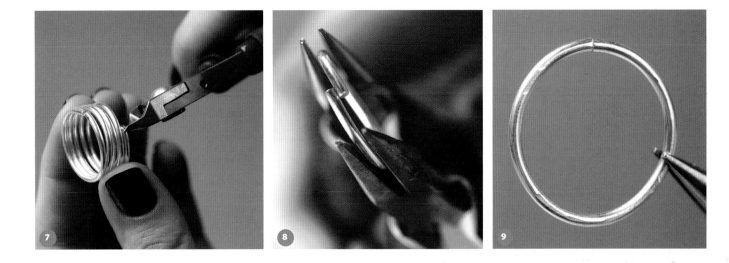

Step 6: The cut that is left on the coil is not flush **(Figure 6)**. In order to cut another ring, flip the cutters back to the original position and trim the sharp point off **(Figure 7)**.

Step 7: You can now flip the cutters over and cut the next ring loose. Every ring you cut requires 2 cuts. There is no cheating here— you must make sure both sides of all rings are flush!

Step 8: Once you have mastered the perfect flush cut, it's time to learn how to correctly close this ring. Using 2 pairs of chain-nose pliers, push the 2 sides of the ring until they overlap slightly **(Figure 8)**.

Step 9: Close the ring until it is perfectly flush, by ever so slightly pulling back on at least 1 end of the ring. Because of the overlap, this applies pressure from the 2 sides of the ring onto the joint, forcing it tightly closed **(Figure 9)**.

Step 10: Repeat Steps 5–9 to make a second ring.

Here is a ring that just won't cut it.

TOOLS AND EQUIPMENT

Stainless-steel work surface

Firebrick

Butane microtorch

Quenching bowl

Hot-pliers

YOU'LL NEED:

Jump rings:

Two 20mm (inner diameter), 14 gauge
(cut in the previous practice on page 23)

Need to Know

Making the cut (page 23)

PRACTICE: Fusing a Ring

Step 1: Place 1 ring flat on the firebrick, which should be sitting on a stainless-steel work surface. There comes a point during the fusing process when it is important to know exactly where the joint is. I always place my joint at the 12 o'clock position. I recommend you place your ring on the firebrick with the joint in the same place each time you fuse.

Step 2: Fire up your torch and start heating your ring. To determine how far your torch should be from your ring, look at the flame. The hottest point is just past the bright blue cone, which is where you want your ring to be. Evenly distribute the heat on all sides of the ring by moving your torch over your ring, going around and around the ring at a steady pace.

Step 3: When the metal starts to look slippery or "flowy" (like liquid), wiggle the torch back and forth over the joint until the ring fuses together. Pull the torch away, set it down, and turn it off **(Figure 1)**.

Step 4: Using your hot-pliers, pick up the ring and drop it in the quenching bowl.

Step 5: Repeat Steps 1–4 and fuse a second ring.

TECHNIQUE: Fusing a Large Circle

Working with large circles or heavy gauges of fine silver wire can prove to be quite a challenge. A small handheld butane torch can only get so hot; there are limitations to how large of a circle you can fuse with this small torch. The previously pictured microtorch burns about 2,100 degrees Fahrenheit. Every torch will vary slightly in the amount of heat it puts out. The best way to work with large circles is to remember that patience is a virtue. I'm not being flip. Make sure you *evenly* distribute your heat around the entire circle, working just past the tip of the bright blue cone. It is especially important when you are working with large circles to maintain even heat distribution. If your heat is not even, the colder parts of the wire will draw the heat away from the hot spots, making fusing very difficult. If you have been trying to close any circle for more than a couple of minutes, chances are that your ring is probably outside the fusing range of your torch.

PRACTICE: Hammering Metal

Step 1: Place a ring flat on your bench block. Using the flat side, hammer until the ring is flattened (**Figure 1**).

Step 2: Using the round end of the hammer, texture your ring until you are satisfied (**Figure 2**). Repeat Steps 1 and 2 for second ring.

TIP: When you are hammering, instead of beating up your fingers, hold the ring to the side of your bench block with a pair of chain-nose pliers.

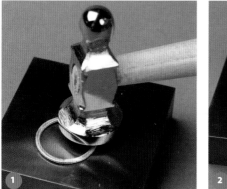

TOOLS AND EQUIPMENT
Bench block
Chasing hammer
Chain-nose pliers

YOU'LL NEED:
Fused rings:
    Two 20mm (inner diameter), 14 gauge
    (from previous step on page 26)

Need to Know
    Making the cut (page 23)
    Fusing a ring (page 26)

Make It: Cha-Cha Earrings
(page 34)

PRACTICE: Tumbling and Professional Finishing

Step 1: Place your fused, hammered rings in the barrel-shaped tumbler, along with your stainless-steel shot. Add 2–3 drops of Dawn dishwashing liquid. Fill with water .5–1" (1.3–2.5 cm) above the stainless-steel shot. Seal with first lid. Place metal lid, washer, and nut on the tumbler. Screw tightly closed. Place the tumbler on the base and plug in.

Step 2: Tumble for 30 minutes.

Step 3: Unplug and remove the tumbler from the base. Open and pour the contents into a fine strainer and rinse. Fish out your rings and allow to dry completely on a cloth or paper towel.

TOOLS AND EQUIPMENT
Tumbler
1-pound (.5 kg) stainless-steel jewelry
    shot
Dawn dishwashing liquid
Fine strainer

YOU'LL NEED:
Fused rings:
    Two 20mm, 14 gauge (from previous step
    above)

TOOLS AND EQUIPMENT
Firebrick

Chain-nose pliers

PRACTICE: Basic Chain

In order to create chain, you have to do a little digging in your firebrick. The ring you are trying to fuse must always be flat on the brick. If not, you will have a difficult time fusing perfect and pretty rings. What this means is that when you join a fused ring to the ring that you are about to fuse, you need to create a "valley" for it to sit in; otherwise, your unfused ring will not lay flat. Make sure any valleys you are digging in your brick are both wide and deep enough to accommodate the rings attached to the ring you are fusing.

DIGGING OUT YOUR BRICK

Step 1: Using chain-nose pliers, scratch at the surface of your brick **(Figure 1)**.

Step 2: When you have dug a valley to your size satisfaction, brush away excess brick dust.

FUSING CHAIN

Step 1:   Cut, close, and fuse 2 rings individually.

Step 2:   Cut a new ring. Attach 2 closed rings to 1 open ring (**Figure 2**). Close the ring.

Step 3:   Place 2 closed rings, standing upright, in the firebrick valley. Lay flat the one you are going to fuse, remembering to take note of where the joint is (**Figure 3**).

Step 4:   Heat in a circular motion until the metal starts to look "flowy." Wiggle on joint until it fuses (**Figure 4**).

Step 5:   Remove heat and, using your hot-pliers, pick up the links and drop in the quenching bowl.

Step 6:   Continue in this fashion until you have the length of chain you desire.

TOOLS AND EQUIPMENT

Tronex razor flush wire cutters

Stainless-steel work surface

Firebrick

Butane microtorch

Hot-pliers

Quenching bowl

YOU'LL NEED:

12 mm mandrel (a standard Sharpie is perfect)

14-gauge fine silver wire

Need to Know

Making the cut (page 23)

Fusing a ring (page 26)

Make It: Arm Candy Oval Bracelet (page 38)

2

3

4

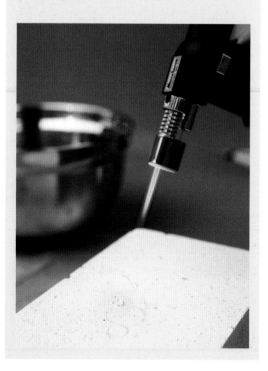

PRACTICE: Fusing and Assembling Fine Silver

Step 1: Carefully cut 1 small ring and place flat on brick.

Step 2: Keep the torch farther away from the ring than when you are working with a heavier gauge. A finer gauge will melt quickly if you hold the flame too close. Finding a happy medium between how close and too close takes a little bit of practice so be prepared to suffer some silver losses. Hold your torch at different heights until you find the perfect heat for the gauge with which you are working.

Step 3: Heat until the metal becomes "flowy." Wiggle on joint. This will happen very quickly, in just a split second, so be careful not to wiggle too much.

Step 4: Once fused, remove the heat, pick up your ring with your hot-pliers, and drop in quenching bowl.

TIP: Something to consider is joining the rings into chain. If you take your torch in a full circle over the rings in the valley, you are likely to get these rings too hot, and they will fuse to the ring you are closing. When working with wire finer than 14 gauge, move your torch in a C shape over the ring. Starting from one side of the rings, work around the top of the ring you are closing, back to the rings in the valley without actually pointing your flame directly at the rings. This will help keep the rings cooler and prevent them from fusing.

PRACTICE: Fusing and Assembling Different Sizes

Assembling rings that are different sizes can get a little tricky. When you are designing pieces of jewelry, think all the way through your design. Start with the smallest rings, and then work up to the largest ones. It is more difficult to fuse small rings with other rings inside of them than it is to fuse the larger ones. Working from smallest to largest will help you have a higher fusing success rate.

PRACTICE: Fusing with Cubic Zirconia Beads

Cubic Zirconia (CZ) is a synthetic diamond. It is strong enough to be able to withstand heating. When you are working with cubic zirconia, it is essential that the change in temperature for the stone is not too fast. If the bead is heated too quickly, it will break. This is called thermal shock. By the same token, if you took a red-hot cubic zirconia bead and dropped it in a bowl full of water, it would cool too rapidly and break. *Do not quench anything you have fused with cubic zirconia.* Make sure you allow plenty of time for your wire and bead to cool before you attempt to touch it.

On the side of your torch, you will see a gas flow adjustment. Usually marked with a +/– sign, you will want to make sure it is turned down as far as it will go before starting this project. Not only can the cubic zirconia not take the heat, the 22-gauge wire you will be working with is so fine it is very easy to overheat.

Step 1:   Place a rondelle on a ring. Gently close this ring using 2 pairs of chain-nose pliers.

Step 2:   Dig a very shallow valley in your brick that will accommodate the small rondelle and not pull the ring up off of the brick.

Step 3:   Warm up the CZ bead by very gently and gradually "dusting" the bead with the flame.

Step 4:   Once the bead is warm, work in a large C shape on the wire until it fuses **(Figure 1)**.

Step 5:   Allow bead and wire to cool before touching them.

TOOLS AND EQUIPMENT

9 mm mandrel

Tronex razor flush wire cutters

2 pairs chain-nose pliers

Stainless-steel work surface

Firebrick

Butane microtorch

Hot-pliers

YOU'LL NEED:

Fused rings:
   Two 9mm rings, 22 gauge
One 4mm cubic zirconia rondelle, black
1 cubic zirconia briolette, black

Need to Know

Make It: Black Tie Cubic Zirconia Necklace (page 46)

Be Prepared!

When you are first working with cubic zirconia beads, it is very easy to destroy the beads by heating or cooling them too quickly. Keep this in mind with any project that you are working on. Buying an extra bead or two as backup is something that I highly recommend. Don't be discouraged; believe me, I broke a lot of beads honing my technique.

WORKING WITH A BRIOLETTE

Step 1: Place a CZ briolette on a new ring. Dig a shallow long valley that will accommodate the briolette.

Step 2: Heat the briolette gradually, 2 times as gradually as the rondelle. Even heating of the bead is the trick to not breaking it. Briolettes are a special case because the hole is so close to the tip of the bead. If you are not careful to keep the whole bead hot, the tip of the bead will snap off **(Figure 1)**.

Step 3: Once the bead is warm, pass the flame along the wire a couple of times and then along the length of the briolette a couple of times **(Figure 2)**.

Step 4: Continue rotating between heating the wire and heating the bead until the wire fuses.

Step 5: Allow bead and wire to cool before touching them.

CHAPTER THREE

Putting It All Together

Have you mastered the basic techniques? Are you eager to start making some jewelry? Incorporate all the skills you've learned and craft some truly unique and professional jewelry. The projects in this chapter are designed to go hand in hand with the techniques in the previous chapter, helping you practice and hone your fusing skills. The best part? Not only do you get to practice your newfound fusing skills, you will also walk away from this chapter with some exciting new baubles that your friends won't believe you made yourself!

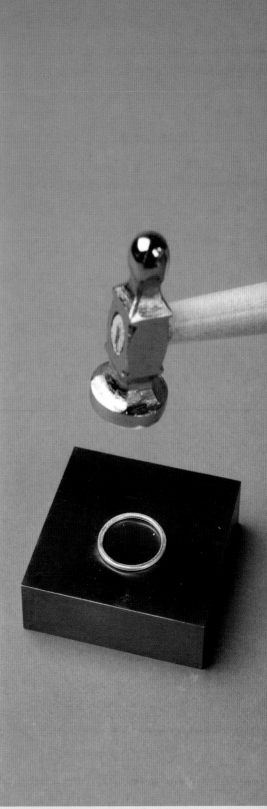

Cha-Cha Earrings

These flirty earrings are the perfect project when you are learning to fuse. Use the components you made while practicing and assemble them into gorgeous earrings that are sure to put you at the center of attention (where we all know you belong).

TOOLS AND EQUIPMENT

Chain-nose pliers
Round-nose pliers
Wire cutters (any will do)

YOU'LL NEED:

Fused rings:
    Two 20mm, 14 gauge (from previous step on page 26)
Ten 24-gauge ball head pins (that you made on page 22)
10 assorted beads. Pictured here:
    Two 8×12mm Swarovski crystal polygon beads, smoked topaz; four 8mm Swarovski crystal bicone beads, fuchsia; four 6mm Swarovski crystal round beads, golden shadow
1 pair sterling silver ear wires

Need to Know

Wire wrapping a loop (page 118)
Attaching an ear wire (page 118)

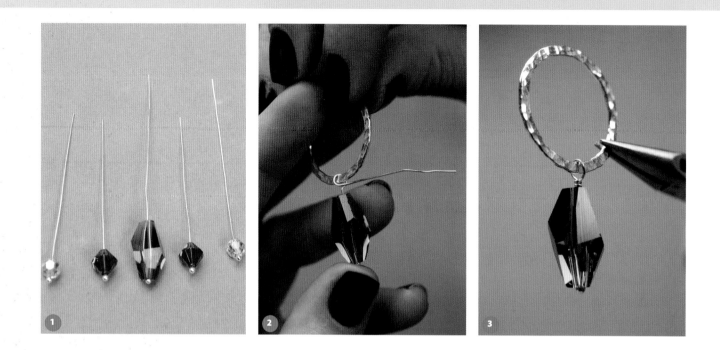

Step 1:   Place a bead on your ball head pin **(Figure 1)**. Form a wire-wrapped loop.

Step 2:   Before closing the loop, attach the head pin to a fused ring **(Figure 2)**.

Step 3:   Wrap loop and trim excess wire **(Figure 3)**.

Step 4:   Repeat for other 4 beads on first earring. Now, with the remaining 5 beads, repeat Steps 1–4 for the second earring.

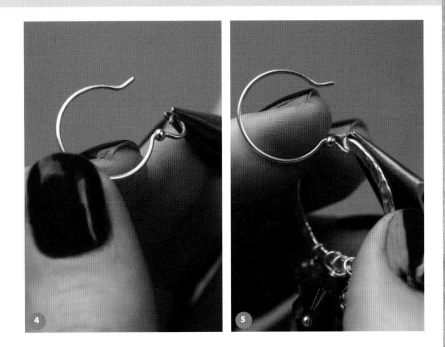

Step 5: Using your chain-nose pliers, twist open the loop on an ear wire **(Figure 4)**.

Step 6: Attach fused ring and close the loop **(Figure 5)**. Repeat for second earring.

Arm Candy Oval Bracelet

Making chain is fun and easy. *Seriously*. This bracelet is sure to go with everything from jeans to your favorite dress. With this super-cute project, you'll learn to shape a round link to add personality to your jewelry. As an added touch, pick out a fun clasp and bauble to allow your style to shine!

TOOLS AND EQUIPMENT

12 mm mandrel

Tronex razor flush wire cutters

Stainless-steel work surface

Firebrick

Butane microtorch

Hot-pliers

Quenching bowl

Chain-nose pliers

Chasing hammer

Tumbler and stainless-steel shot

YOU'LL NEED:

Fused rings:
  Eleven 12mm, 14 gauge

Two 6mm heavy sterling silver open jump
  rings

1 clasp. Pictured: 11×23mm sterling silver
  oval lobster claw

1 bead or dangle. Pictured: 27mm
  Swarovski rhodium-plated filigree
  pendant, pretty

Need to Know

Making the cut (page 23)

Fusing a ring (page 26)

Basic chain (page 28)

Hammering metal (page 27)

Tumbling (page 27)

Step 1: Close and fuse 6 rings separately.

Step 2: Using the remaining 5 open rings, join these rings into a chain.

Step 3: Place the tips of your chain-nose pliers inside of a link, centered across from each other **(Figure 1)**.

Step 4: Gently pull the tips of the pliers apart until you get an oval **(Figure 2)**. Shape all of the rings in this manner.

Step 5: Now it's time to hammer the links flat. Take the first ring and hold the rings linked to it off to the side. Hammer half of the first ring flat. Do not texture **(Figure 3)**!

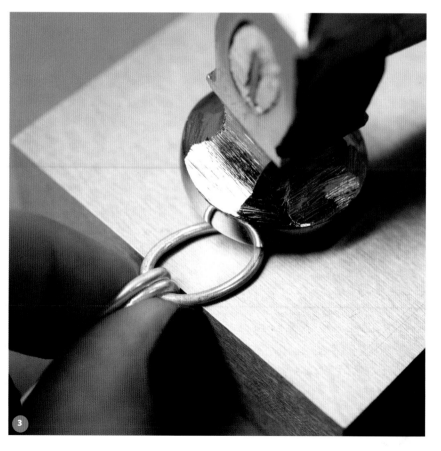

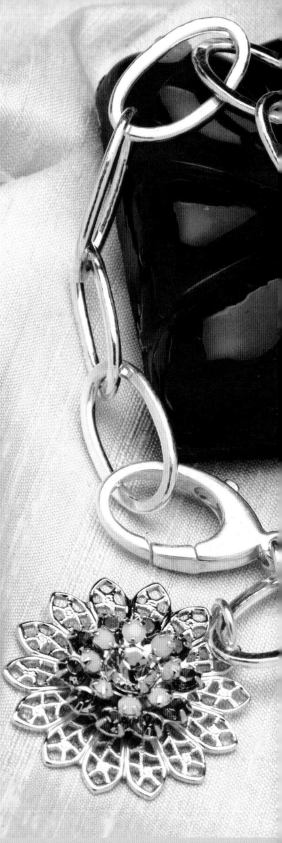

Step 6:   Turn the ring 180 degrees and hammer the other half flat. Hammer the rest of the rings in this manner **(Figure 4)**.

Step 7:   Tumble for 30 minutes.

Step 8:   Using chain-nose pliers, open a sterling jump ring and attach the clasp. Open the second jump ring and attach the pendant. Using additional jump rings or head pins (depending on the bead you select), attach the clasp and bead to the same end link on your bracelet.

Wormhole Earrings

As an avid horror and sci-fi movie fan, these playful earrings make me think of wormholes in the space-time continuum. The dimension and movement when worn make them look like an optical illusion dangling from your earlobes. Not only are these spectacular earrings, but they offer a good opportunity to practice assembling rings of various sizes.

TOOLS AND EQUIPMENT
5 mm, 8 mm, 11 mm, 18 mm mandrels
Tronex razor flush wire cutters
Stainless-steel work surface
Firebrick
Butane microtorch
Hot-pliers
Quenching bowl
Chain-nose pliers

YOU'LL NEED:
Fused rings:
    Small: Twelve 5mm, 18 gauge
    Medium-small: Six 8mm, 18 gauge
    Medium-large: Six 11mm, 18 gauge
    Large: Six 14mm, 18 gauge
1 pair sterling silver ear wires

Need to Know

    Making the cut (page 23)
    Fusing a ring (page 26)
    Tumbling (page 27)
    Basic chain (page 28)
    Fusing and assembling fine silver (page 30)
    Fusing fine gauges (page 30)
    Attaching an ear wire (page 118)

Step 1: Cut 6 small jump rings and fuse separately.

Step 2: Join 1 small ring to each of the small closed rings. Make sure to work back and forth in a C shape when you are fusing this ring. Continue in this manner for all small rings **(Figure 1)**.

Step 3: Join and fuse 1 medium-small ring to 1 small ring on each set of 2. Repeat 5 times **(Figure 2)**.

Step 4: Attach 1 medium-large ring to the same small ring to which you fused the medium-small ring in Step 3. Repeat 5 times, so that you have 6 clusters with a small, medium-small, and medium-large ring attached to 1 small ring **(Figure 3)**.

Step 5: Join 2 ring clusters together by linking 1 large jump ring through 2 of the small jump rings holding the other 3 fused rings. In other words, you are linking 2 clusters together by fusing 1 large jump ring to 2 clusters **(Figure 4)**.

Step 6: Join another large jump ring to the small jump ring on the bottom cluster, and attach a third cluster for the third tier **(Figure 5)**.

Step 7: Attach 1 large jump ring to the bottom cluster and fuse to complete the pattern **(Figure 6)**.

Step 8: Repeat Steps 5–7 for second earring. With chain-nose pliers, attach ear wire and tumble for 45–60 minutes.

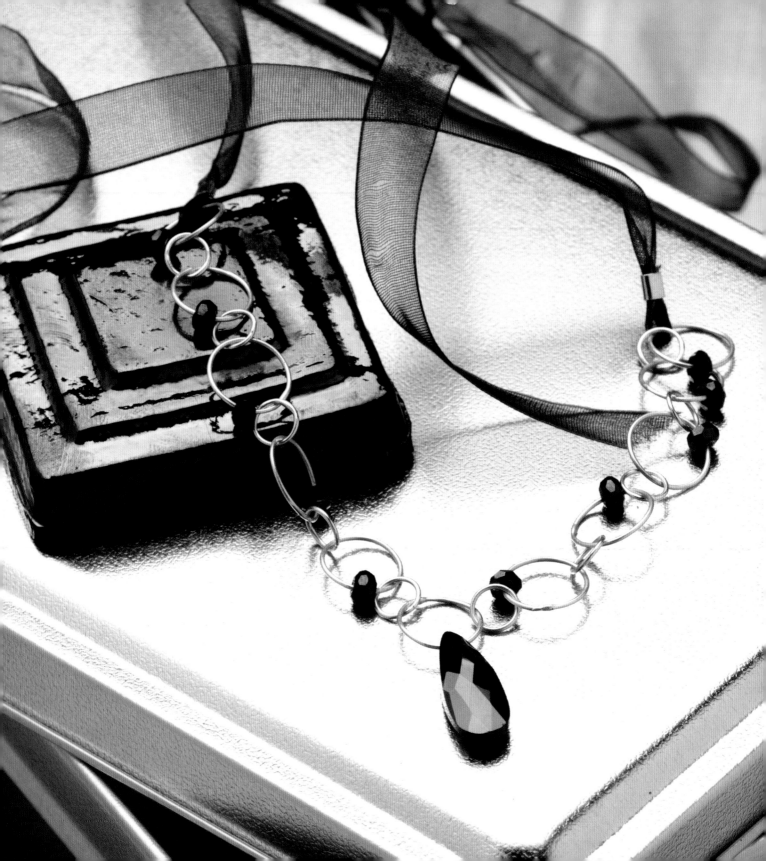

Black Tie Cubic Zirconia Necklace

Charming and sweet, this adjustable necklace—sparkling with a cubic zirconia teardrop—will add elegance to any outfit. I like using organza ribbon or cord to end a necklace. You can tie it at any length to go with anything in your wardrobe!

TOOLS AND EQUIPMENT

4 mm, 9 mm mandrels
Tronex razor flush wire cutters
Stainless-steel work surface
Firebrick
Butane microtorch
Hot-pliers
Tumbler and stainless-steel shot
Chain-nose or crimping pliers

YOU'LL NEED:

Fused rings:
    Small: Ten 4mm, 22 gauge
    Large: Eleven 9mm, 22 gauge
Ten 4mm cubic zirconia rondelles
One 7×18mm cubic zirconia briolette, black
Two 36" (91.4 cm) pieces of organza ribbon, black
Two 3x3mm sterling silver crimp beads

Need to Know

    Fusing a ring (page 26)
    Tumbling (page 27)
    Basic chain (page 28)
    Making the cut (page 28)
    Fusing with cubic zirconia beads (page 31)
    Crimping (page 118)

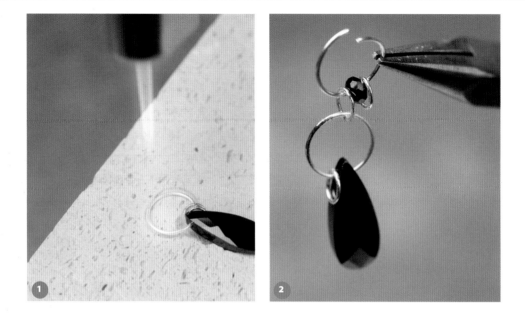

Step 1: Cut, close, and fuse 10 small jump rings.

Step 2: Place the briolette and 2 small rings on one of the large rings and fuse large ring **(Figure 1)**.

Step 3: Slip a rondelle and a small ring on another large ring; attach this large ring to one of the small rings on the large ring you fused in Step 2. Fuse large ring **(Figure 2)**.

Step 4: Repeat 3 times.

Step 5: Add 1 large ring with a rondelle and fuse to the last small ring on this side. Allow beads and wire to cool completely before touching.

Step 6: Repeat Steps 3–6 for the other side.

Step 7: Tumble for 30 minutes.

Step 8: Crimp one 36" (91.4 cm) length of organza ribbon onto the last link on either side.

CHAPTER FOUR

Taking It to the Next Level

Now that you have learned the basics, and mastered them creating some basic projects, it's time to step it up a notch. The projects in this chapter are designed to help you think outside of the box. All of the fundamentals are here, but there are some fun new twists thrown in as well!

Just in case you don't love the colors or beads used in the projects that follow, don't feel like you have to make them exactly as shown! Use the designs as inspiration for your own fusing style and make the pieces presented here your own. The beads and other components featured are all things I would pick for *my* jewelry—you can always pick different colors or beads to add your own flavor to the projects!

Heart Attack Hammered Bracelet

This sweet bracelet is a totally cute alternative to the standard round-link bracelet. While your fused creations are always a gift to give yourself, this piece is a perfect gift for loved ones (or people you really like a lot).

TOOLS AND EQUIPMENT

6 mm, 12 mm mandrels

Tronex razor flush wire cutters

Stainless-steel work surface

Firebrick

Butane microtorch

Hot-pliers

Quenching bowl

Chain-nose pliers

Chasing hammer

Bench block

Tumbler and stainless-steel shot

YOU'LL NEED:

Fused rings:

    Small: Six 6mm, 16 gauge

    Large: Seven 12mm, 14 gauge

Two 6mm sterling silver jump rings

1 clasp. Pictured: 13×19mm sterling silver figure-eight lobster claw

Need to Know

    Making the cut (page 23)

    Fusing a ring (page 26)

    Hammering metal (page 27)

    Tumbling (page 27)

    Basic chain (page 28)

Step 1:   Close and fuse all of the small jump rings.

Step 2:   Create chain by joining all of the small rings together using the large rings. Attach 1 large ring on either end of the chain, so you have 7 large rings joined together by 6 small rings.

Step 3:   Using chain-nose pliers, place the tips inside 1 large ring. Make sure the tips are centered in the ring and then gently pry the tips apart, elongating your ring until it is an oval **(Figure 1)**.

Step 4:   Using a second pair of chain-nose pliers, grasp the center of the long side of the oval with both pairs of pliers.

Step 5:   Bend both pairs of pliers downward and toward each other, creating a V shape **(Figure 2)**.

Step 6:   Graspthe bottom of the oval directly under the "V" with both pairs of pliers and bend downward, creating another V **(Figure 3)**.

Step 7: Gently squeeze along the flattened parts of the heart, smoothing out any bends in the wire. Pay close attention to the tips of the V shapes, making them as pointed as possible **(Figure 4)**.

Step 8: Place the tips of 1 pair of chain-nose pliers centered in 1 of the small rings. Gently pry the tips open, elongating the ring into an oval.

Step 9: Repeat Steps 3–7 for each of the large rings and Step 8 for each of the small rings until all of the rings have been shaped.

Step 10: Using a chasing hammer and bench block, hammer flat and then texture all of the large rings.

Step 11: Using a sterling jump ring (open by using a pair of chain-nose pliers), attach a clasp of your choice.

Step 12: Tumble for 30 minutes.

Livin' Large Hammered Pendant

This charming necklace is a good way to use your favorite beads to accent a bold pendant. Flowers and butterflies not your thing? Use your imagination and select any beads you like. This project makes a great gift for just about anyone and is great practice for working with large gauges of wire.

TOOLS AND EQUIPMENT

8 mm, 19 mm, 27 mm mandrels

Wire cutters (I recommend Lindstrom or horse cutters)

Stainless-steel work surface

Firebrick

Butane microtorch

Quenching bowl

Hot-pliers

2 pairs chain-nose pliers

Chasing hammer

Bench block

Tumbler and stainless-steel shot

Crimping pliers (optional)

YOU'LL NEED:

Fused rings:

Small: One 8mm, 12 gauge

Medium: One 19mm, 12 gauge

Large: One 27mm, 12 gauge

One hundred sixty 2mm Swarovski crystal round beads, silver shade

Six 5mm Swarovski crystal butterfly beads, fuchsia

One 14mm Swarovski crystal flower pendant, fuchsia

Two 6mm sterling silver open jump rings

24 inches (61 cm) of .014 Soft Flex

Two 2×2mm sterling silver crimp beads

1 hook-and-eye clasp. Pictured: 24×9mm sterling silver flower hook-and-eye clasp

Need to Know

Fusing a ring (page 26)

Hammering metal (page 27)

Tumbling (page 27)

Basic chain (page 28)

Crimping (page 118)

Step 1: Cut and fuse 1 small ring.

Step 2: Cut and join medium ring to small ring, and fuse medium ring **(Figure 1)**.

Step 3: Cut and join large ring to small ring, and fuse large ring **(Figure 2)**.

Step 4: Using 2 pairs of chain-nose pliers, grab 1 side of the large ring and bend it into a V **(Figure 3)**.

Step 5: Gently elongate the rounded side of the ring by gently pushing the ring together, creating a teardrop shape **(Figure 4)**.

Step 6: With the tips of your chain-nose pliers, squeeze close to the V to sharpen up the point and then straighten out the sides of the teardrop by gently squeezing along the wire with your chain-nose pliers **(Figure 5)**.

Step 7: In the same way, shape the medium ring into a teardrop.

Step 8: Hammer the 2 large rings flat and texture.

Step 9: Tumble for 30 minutes.

Step 10: Using chain-nose pliers, attach a flower bead to a sterling jump ring **(Figure 6)**.

Step 11: Using a second sterling silver jump ring, attach the flower bead to the small ring on your fused pendant so it hangs in the center **(Figure 7)**.

Step 12: String beads on Soft Flex. To make the pattern pictured, string thirty 3mm crystals and one 5mm butterfly; twenty 3mm crystals and one 5mm butterfly 2 times; string twenty 3mm crystals, slip the pendant onto your necklace, and string one 5mm butterfly; string twenty 3mm crystals and one 5mm butterfly 2 times; string thirty 3mm crystals.

Step 13: Using crimp beads, attach clasp to each end of Soft Flex.

TOOLS AND EQUIPMENT

Ring mandrel

Wire cutters (I recommend Lindstrom or horse cutters)

Stainless-steel work surface

Firebrick

Butane microtorch

Hot-pliers

Quenching bowl

Tumbler and stainless-steel shot

Chain-nose pliers

YOU'LL NEED:

6" (15.2 cm) of 12-gauge fine silver wire

12" (30.5 cm) of 22-gauge sterling silver half-hard wire

One 3mm Swarovski crystal round bead, crystal

One 16mm Swarovski crystal square button, crystal sage

Need to Know

Making the cut (page 23)

Fusing a ring (page 26)

Tumbling (page 27)

Sizing formulas for rings (page 59)

Coiled, Embellished, and Hammered Rings

Blingin' Button Ring

Making rings for your fingers can prove to be quite a challenge. Making sure the ring turns out the right size every single time can be very frustrating. The formulas on the previous page are guidelines to follow that will help your rings fit perfectly every time. Due to variations in how tightly you wrap your wire or your specific cutting technique, you may need to slightly alter the formulas to make them work perfectly for you. The next three projects will show you different techniques so you can create rings for any occasion or for every finger.

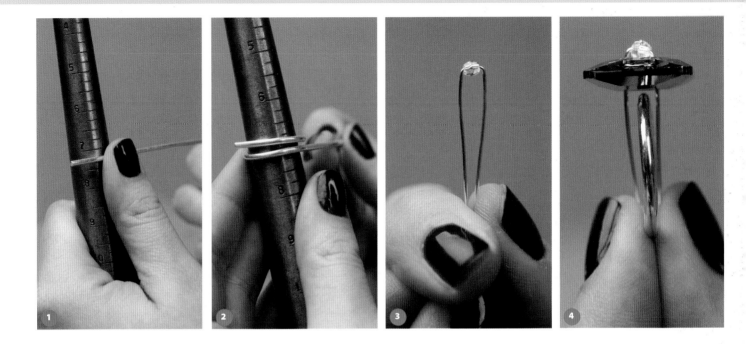

Step 1: Using the sizing formula on page 59, wrap your 12-gauge wire around the ring mandrel, taking care to place it around the mandrel in the correct spot to make the size you need **(Figures 1 and 2)**.

Step 2: Cut and fuse the ring.

Step 3: Tumble for 1 hour.

Step 4: Place 3mm bead in the center of 22-gauge wire and bend both ends of the wire down, creating a U shape, with the 3mm bead in the center of the U **(Figure 3)**.

Step 5: Place 1 end of the wire through each hole of the button.

Step 6: Place the ring in the center of the 2 pieces of wire coming out the back of the button **(Figure 4)**.

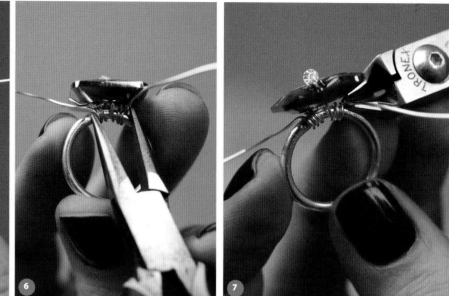

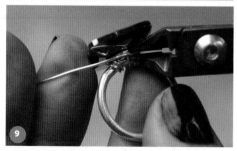

Step 7: Coil 1 end in one direction around the band of the ring 3 times. Coil the other end in the opposite direction around the band of the ring 3 times (**Figure 5**).

Step 8: Using your chain-nose pliers, squish coils together so they are hidden under the button (**Figure 6**).

Step 9: Trim 1 end of the wire on the outside of the band (**Figure 7**).

Step 10: Wrap the other end of the wire underneath the button and around the wire coming out of the button 3–4 times or until button is snug and no longer wiggly (**Figure 8**).

Step 11: Trim wire and, using your chain-nose pliers, tuck the ends under the button (**Figures 9 and 10**).

Textured Band

To ensure your textured band will turn out the right size, pay attention when you are hammering! The ring will stretch very quickly as you hammer, and you have to make it all the way around the band before the ring is too large. Hammer lightly until you get a good idea of how quickly it will stretch. Once you've made one, create a few more to stack on a finger and even consider flanking your smooth band with two textured bands for maximum impact.

TOOLS AND EQUIPMENT

Wire cutters (I recommend Lindstrom or horse cutters)
Stainless-steel work surface
Firebrick
Butane microtorch
Hot-pliers
Quenching bowl
Chasing hammer
Bench block
Tumbler and stainless-steel shot

YOU'LL NEED:
6" (15.2 cm) of 10-gauge fine silver wire

Need to Know

Making the cut (page 23)
Fusing a ring (page 26)
Hammering metal (page 27)
Tumbling (page 27)
Sizing formulas for rings (page 59)

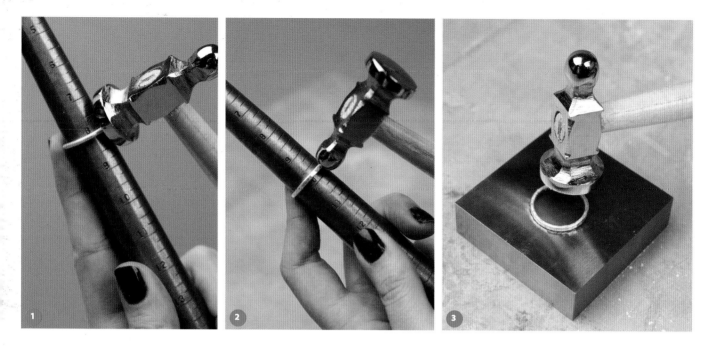

Step 1: Using the sizing formula on page 67, wrap the wire around the mandrel.

Step 2: Cut and fuse the ring.

Step 3: Place on ring mandrel. Hammer lightly around the band with the flat side of the chasing hammer until it is 1 size smaller than desired finished size **(Figure 1)**.

Step 4: Turn hammer over and, using the ball end, lightly hammer until the ring is the desired size **(Figure 2)**.

Step 5: Place it on bench block and hammer flat any unevenness **(Figure 3)**.

Step 6: Tumble for 30 minutes. To make this ring using 12-gauge wire, use the sizing formula on page 59 and repeat all of the hammering instructions.

Coiled Ring

The next step after making a basic ring is to funk it up. For a bit more edge, create this big chunky coil. And because we all have different preferences and tastes, I've included three variations so you can pick the one that suits you best.

TIP: Heavy gauges of wire will not ball with just a torch, such as your 24-gauge head pins. There is not enough heat to ball heavy gauges of wire. In order to make a ball on heavy wire, we will need to use our brick. The downside to doing this is that one side of the ball will be flat. Fortunately, this actually is to our advantage for this particular project. Since the back of the ball will be flat, the ring will actually lay better on your finger. I recommend doing a practice run with this technique so you can get used to how the metal will move before you work on your actual ring project.

TOOLS AND EQUIPMENT

Wire cutters (I recommend Lindstrom or horse cutters)

Stainless-steel work surface

Firebrick

Butane microtorch

Hot-pliers

Quenching bowl

Brass measuring gauge or ruler

Metal file

Ring mandrel

Polishing cloth

Chasing hammer

Tumbler and stainless-steel shot

YOU'LL NEED:

10-gauge fine silver wire

Need to Know

Tumbling (page 27)

Sizing formulas for rings (page 59)

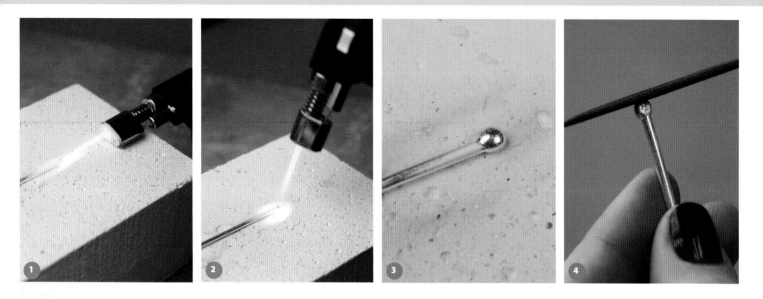

Step 1: Using the sizing formula on page 59, cut wire to the correct length.

Step 2: Place the wire flat on the brick. Pass the flame along the length of the wire a couple of times to warm it up.

Step 3: Lay the torch flat on the end of the brick, aiming the flame down the core of the wire. Keep heating until the metal begins to glow slightly at the end of the wire **(Figure 1)**.

Step 4: Rotating on an axis, tip the flame up so it is directly above the wire. This will pull the ball down the length of wire **(Figure 2)**.

Step 5: Lay the torch back in the flat position and heat the core of the wire to round the ball back out.

Step 6: Repeat Steps 3–5 until you make a 6mm ball **(Figure 3)**.

Step 7: Repeat Steps 2–6 on the other end of the wire.

Step 8:   Timeto take a look at the ball. If there are any sharp points or unevenness, now is the time to take care of it. Any cleanup should be done before the ring is wrapped and tumbled. Use a small metal file to remove any sharp spots **(Figure 4)**.

SHAPING THE RING

Step 1: Begin wrapping the wire around the ring mandrel ½ size smaller than the desired finished size by placing 1 ball under your thumb and wrapping the wire down the mandrel and underneath the ball **(Figures 1 and 2)**.

Step 2: In order to make sure all of the coils are the same size, shift the ring up slightly on the mandrel and wrap the next coil, again ½ size smaller than the desired finished size **(Figure 3)**.

Step 3: Pull the ring off the mandrel. Gently pry the coils apart and shape the coil **(Figure 4)**.

Step 4: Place the ring back on the mandrel, cover with a polishing cloth, and gently tap each ball with the flat side of your hammer so it will curve around the mandrel and lay flat against your finger **(Figures 5 and 6)**. If you do not cover the ball with a polishing cloth before you hammer, you will end up putting hammer marks on the metal instead of it being nice and smooth.

Step 5: Tumble for 1 hour.

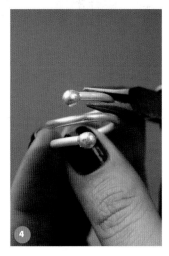

Blingin' Button Ring

Textured Band

Coiled Ring

Sizing Formulas for Rings

All of the formulas listed are basic guidelines for sizing rings. Variations in your particular technique may cause your ring to be a slightly different size. How tightly you wrap the wire around the ring mandrel and how close your cuts are on your coil will affect the final size of the ring. Before you make a bunch of rings, try it out and see if you need to vary any of these formulas.

Smooth Band (for Blingin' Button Ring): ½ to ¾ of a size smaller than desired finished size.

Textured Band: 12-gauge wire: 2½ sizes smaller than desired finished size. 10-gauge wire: 3½ sizes smaller than desired finished size.

Coiled Band: It takes about ¼ inch (.6 cm) of wire to create a ball that is 6mm in size. This formula is broken down at right to help you determine how to make a ring larger or smaller.

Half Coil

DESIRED FINISHED SIZE	LENGTH		TOTAL LENGTH TO CUT
5	2¼" (5.7 cm)	+ ½" (1.3 cm) (BALL) =	2¾" (7 cm)
6	2⅜" (6 cm)	+ ½" (1.3 cm) (BALL) =	2⅞" (7.3 cm)
7	2½" (6.4 cm)	+ ½" (1.3 cm) (BALL) =	3" (7.6 cm)
8	2⅝" (6.7 cm)	+ ½" (1.3 cm) (BALL) =	3⅛" (7.9 cm)
9	2¾" (7 cm)	+ ½" (1.3 cm) (BALL) =	3¼" (8.3 cm)
10	2⅞" (7.3 cm)	+ ½" (1.3 cm) (BALL) =	3⅜" (8.6 cm)
11	3" (7.6 cm)	+ ½" (1.3 cm) (BALL) =	3½" (8.9 cm)

Single Coil

DESIRED FINISHED SIZE	LENGTH		TOTAL LENGTH TO CUT
12	4½" (11.4 cm)	+ ½" (1.3 cm) (BALL) =	5" (12.7 cm)
13	4¾" (12.1 cm)	+ ½" (1.3 cm) (BALL) =	5¼" (13.3 cm)
14	5" (12.7 cm)	+ ½" (1.3 cm) (BALL) =	5½" (14 cm)
15	5¼" (13.3 cm)	+ ½" (1.3 cm) (BALL) =	5¾" (14.6 cm)
16	5½" (14 cm)	+ ½" (1.3 cm) (BALL) =	6" (15.2 cm)
17	5¾" (14.6 cm)	+ ½" (1.3 cm) (BALL) =	6¼" (15.9 cm)
18	6" (15.2 cm)	+ ½" (1.3 cm) (BALL) =	6½" (16.5 cm)

Double Coil

DESIRED FINISHED SIZE	LENGTH		TOTAL LENGTH TO CUT
5	6¾" (17.1 cm)	+ ½" (1.3 cm) (BALL) =	7¼" (18.4 cm)
6	7⅛" (18.1 cm)	+ ½" (1.3 cm) (BALL) =	7⅝" (19.4 cm)
7	7½" (19.1 cm)	+ ½" (1.3 cm) (BALL) =	8" (20.3 cm)
8	7⅞" (20 cm)	+ ½" (1.3 cm) (BALL) =	8⅜" (21.3 cm)
9	8¼" (21 cm)	+ ½" (1.3 cm) (BALL) =	8¾" (22.2 cm)
10	8⅝" (22 cm)	+ ½" (1.3 cm) (BALL) =	9⅛" (23.2 cm)
11	9" (22.9 cm)	+ ½" (1.3 cm) (BALL) =	9½" (24.1 cm)

Angled Dangle Earrings

These marquise-shaped earrings are so lightweight and airy, you won't even remember you are wearing them! The delicate rings swing freely when these earrings are worn, creating lots of playful motion.

TOOLS AND EQUIPMENT

4 mm, 6 mm, 9 mm, 19 mm mandrels

Tronex razor flush wire cutters

Stainless-steel work surface

Firebrick

Butane microtorch

Hot-pliers

Quenching bowl

2 pairs chain-nose pliers

Bench block

Chasing hammer

Sharpie

Tumbler and stainless-steel shot

YOU'LL NEED:

Fused rings:

    Small: Twelve 4mm, 20 gauge

    Medium-small: Two 6mm, 20 gauge; two 6mm, 18 gauge

    Medium: Two 9mm, 20 gauge; two 9mm, 18 gauge

    Large: Two 19mm, 20 gauge; two 19mm, 18 gauge

1 pair sterling silver ear wires

Need to Know

Making the cut (page 23)

Fusing a ring (page 26)

Fusing fine gauges (page 30)

Fusing and assembling different sizes (page 30)

Attaching an ear wire (page 118)

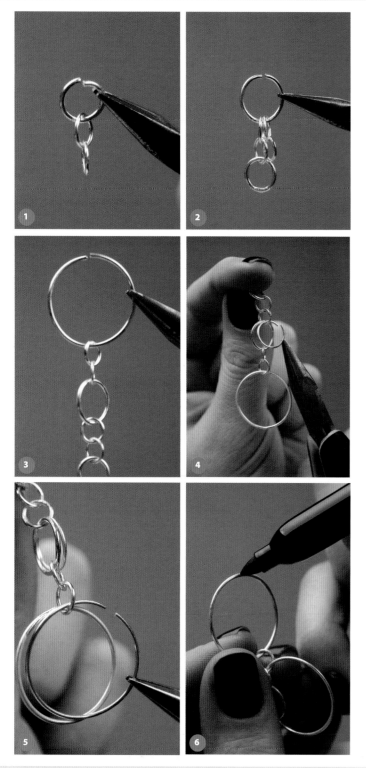

Step 1: Close and fuse 6 small rings.

Step 2: Join and fuse 1 small ring to each of the 6 closed small rings.

Step 3: Join 1 medium-small 18-gauge jump ring to 1 group of 2 small rings (**Figure 1**).

Step 4: Repeat Step 3 for second earring.

Step 5: Join 1 medium 18-gauge ring to the other small ring on the same cluster. Add a second cluster and fuse (**Figure 2**).

Step 6: Repeat Step 5 for second earring.

Step 7: Join 1 large 18-gauge ring to the other small ring on the bottom cluster (**Figure 3**).

Step 8: Repeat for second earring.

Step 9: Join 1 medium 20-gauge jump ring to the same top cluster as the 18-gauge ring (**Figure 4**).

Step 10: Repeat for second earring.

Step 11: Join 1 large 20-gauge jump ring to the bottom cluster (**Figure 5**).

Step 12: Repeat for second earring.

Step 13: Fuse 2 medium-small jump rings separately.

Step 14: On the large 18-gauge ring, mark 2 spots directly across from each other with a Sharpie (**Figures 6 and 7**).

7

8

9

10

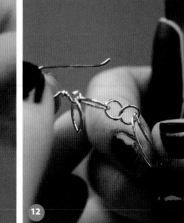

11

12

Step 15: Place chain-nose pliers centered on the marks and pull into an oval **(Figure 8)**.

Step 16: Use 2 pairs of chain-nose pliers; grab the oval on either side of your black marks and shape into a V **(Figure 9)**. Repeat on the other side of the ring.

Step 17: Gently squeeze along the sides to make it more of a marquise shape **(Figures 10 and 11)**.

Step 18: Repeat for other large, medium, and medium-small rings, including the one that was separate.

Step 19: Hammer flat. Attach the top medium jump ring and the loose medium jump ring to an ear wire **(Figure 12)**.

Step 20: Tumble for 45 minutes.

Totally Money Stamped Bracelet

Silver jewelry stamped with words is very popular. Tired of the same choices, I tried to come up with something new and exciting. This classy bracelet will not only make you feel like a million bucks, it also looks like it cost a million bucks!

TOOLS AND EQUIPMENT

8 mm, 19 mm mandrels

Wire cutters (I recommend Lindstrom or horse cutters)

Stainless-steel work surface

Firebrick

Butane microtorch

Hot-pliers

Quenching bowl

Chasing hammer

Bench block

Household hammer

1/16" (.12 cm) letter stamp set

Tumbler and stainless-steel shot

Q-tip

Silver black

Steel wool

Polishing cloth

YOU'LL NEED:

Fused rings:

Small: Five 8mm, 14 gauge

Large: Six 19mm, 12 gauge

1 sterling silver clasp. Pictured: 13mm sterling silver toggle

Two 6mm sterling silver jump rings

Need to Know

Making the cut (page 23)

Fusing a ring (page 26)

Hammering metal (page 27)

Tumbling (page 27)

Basic chain (page 28)

Silver Black: It's Toxic, But Dang It Works Well!

Silver black is a highly toxic hydrochloric acid-based patina. It is very important to know safety information about this product. First, you want to make sure this never comes in contact with your skin. If you do get some on your skin, immediately flush with cold water for 15 minutes and use lots of soap to wash it off. You can further neutralize the acid using baking soda. Silver black is also highly toxic to breathe. Make sure you are using this solution in a well-ventilated room. As with any toxic substance, make sure you keep this out of the reach of children and pets.

Step 1: Close and fuse 5 small rings.

Step 2: Cut 6 large rings. Join all of small rings together with 4 large jump rings and fuse large rings. Join 1 large jump ring to each end and fuse.

Step 3: With a bench block and your chasing hammer, hammer all of the large rings flat. Make sure each is hammered flat enough to accommodate the letters you will be stamping with.

Step 4: Line up the first letter in the center of the flattened wire. Hit once with a household hammer (hammering more than once can leave multiple shadows of the letter). Continue stamping until you have spelled all of your words **(Figure 1)**.

Step 5: Tumble for 30 minutes.

Step 6: Using a Q-tip, apply silver black to the stamped words, taking care not to come into contact with the silver black **(Figure 2)**. Rinse well.

Step 7: Dry thoroughly, then gently brush over the words with steel wool **(Figure 3)**. Note that too much pressure with the steel wool will leave a brushed texture on the metal.

Step 8: Polish with a polishing cloth **(Figure 4)**. If you ever re-tumble this bracelet, you will have to reapply the silver black solution.

TIP: Making a mistake while stamping can prove irritating and costly, so practice letter stamping on an inexpensive surface, such as copper sheet, which you can find at most hardware stores.

Deceptively Simple Necklace

You'll receive endless compliments when you wear this quick and easy necklace. It looks much more impressive than the time it took to whip it up. Destined to become a signature piece, it goes with everything. Pick any bead you want to link the components together.

TOOLS AND EQUIPMENT

5 mm, 10 mm, 17 mm, 27 mm mandrels

Wire cutters (I recommend Lindstrom or horse cutters)

Stainless-steel work surface

Firebrick

Butane microtorch

Hot-pliers

Quenching bowl

Bench block

Chasing hammer

2-hole metal punch

Tumbler and stainless-steel shot

YOU'LL NEED:

Fused rings:

    Small: One 5mm, 12 gauge

    Medium-small: One 10mm, 12 gauge

    Medium-large: One 17mm, 12 gauge

    Large: One 27mm, 12 gauge

12" (30.5 cm) of 22-gauge sterling silver wire

1 bead. Pictured: 12mm nugget fire polished glass, chartreuse

36" (91.4 cm) of 2mm waxed cotton cord

One 3mm sterling silver cord clasp (there should be 2 components: a hook and an eye-cord end)

Need to Know

Making the cut (page 23)

Fusing a ring (page 26)

Hammering metal (page 27)

Tumbling (page 27)

Wire wrapping a loop (page 118)

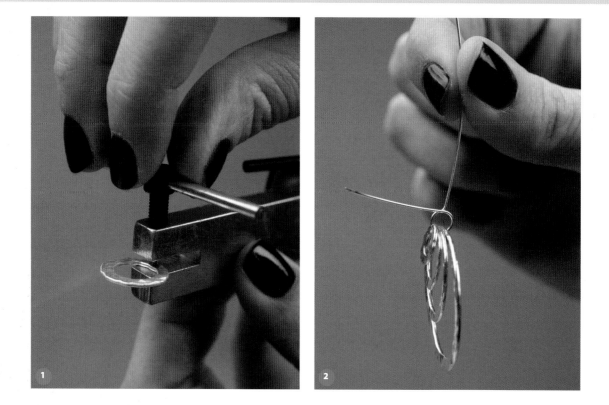

Step 1: Close and fuse all 4 rings separately.

Step 2: Hammer flat and texture.

Step 3: Using the small bit of 2-hole punch, line up in center of flattened wire **(Figure 1)**.

Step 4: Twist the bit down until it punches through the metal. Gently twist the bit back (don't ever pull the metal off; this is likely to break the bit!) until the metal falls off.

Step 5: Tumble all rings for 30 minutes.

Step 6: Join all together with 22-gauge sterling large wire wrap **(Figure 2)**.

Step 7: Add a bead and create a wire-wrapped loop above the bead.

Step 8: Cut cord to length (here: two 18" lengths [45.7 cm]) and insert each end of the cord into a cord clasp. Using the tips of chain-nose pliers, crimp the middle of the clasp. Slip on your fused pendant and repeat crimping for the second half of the clasp **(Figure 3)**.

Shooting Star Earrings

Tie together everything you've learned in these rock star earrings. Mix together chain, Swarovski crystal briolettes, and fused components to create a pair of earrings that your favorite female rocker would be proud to wear but that will also add a little punch to your work wardrobe.

TOOLS AND EQUIPMENT

7 mm, 27 mm mandrels

Tronex razor flush wire cutters

Stainless-steel work surface

Firebrick

Butane microtorch

Hot-pliers

Quenching bowl

2 pairs chain-nose pliers

Bench block

Chasing hammer

Measuring tape

2 Sharpies in different colors

Tumbler and stainless-steel shot

YOU'LL NEED:

Fused rings:

Small: Ten 7mm, 16 gauge

Large: Two 27mm, 16 gauge

24" (61 cm) of sterling silver chain

Pictured: Sterling silver small oval long-and-short chain

10 small briolette beads. Pictured: 7×4mm

Swarovski crystal small briolette pendant, tanzanite

Ten 4mm sterling silver jump rings

Four 6mm sterling silver jump rings

1 pair sterling silver ear wires

Need to Know

Making the cut (page 23)

Fusing a ring (page 26)

Hammering metal (page 27)

Tumbling (page 27)

Attaching an ear wire (page 118)

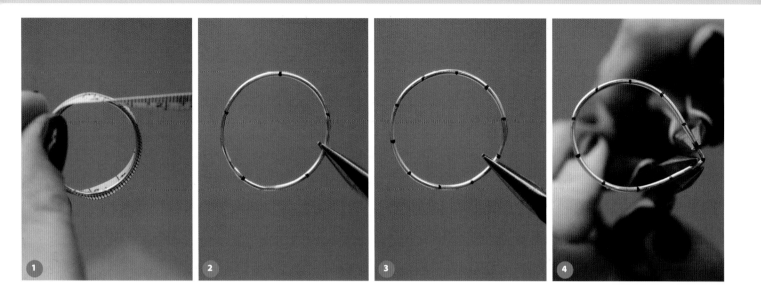

Step 1:   Close and fuse all rings separately.

Step 2:   Measure outer diameter of large ring with tape measure **(Figure 1)**. It should be a total circumference of 95mm. Mark a spot on the ring every 19mm with a Sharpie—5 marks total **(Figure 2)**.

Step 3:   In between each of the 5 marks, mark a spot in the middle with a different color Sharpie—5 more marks total **(Figure 3)**.

Step 4:   Using 2 pairs of chain-nose pliers, start with one of the first color marks and shape a V **(Figure 4)**.

Step 5:   Move to the next mark (second color) and bend in a V in the opposite direction **(Figure 5)**.

Step 6:   Continue around the ring, bending each of the marks in the same direction as the other marks of the same color until you have formed a star **(Figure 6)**. Using your chain-nose pliers, straighten out any bends in the sides of the stars and sharpen up the corners by squeezing on either side of the marks.

Step 7: Hammer flat and texture the star rings.

Step 8: Hammer flat and texture all 10 small rings.

Step 9: Tumble for 30 minutes. The marks from the Sharpie will come off in the tumbler.

Step 10: Cut chain (5 pieces for each earring) in varying lengths. You can decide how long or short you would like your earrings to be. To make the pair pictured, the longest chain is 2¾" (7 cm); next is 2½" (6.4 cm); next is 2¼" (5.7 cm); 1¾" (4.4 cm); 1½" (3.8 cm). Open up a 4mm sterling jump ring and slide on 1 small fused ring and 1 small briolette bead. Attach the jump ring to 1 end of a piece of chain and close jump ring **(Figure 7)**. Repeat 4 times.

Step 11: Using a 6mm jump ring, attach all pieces of chain (using the opposite ends this time) and 1 star together. With a second 6mm sterling jump ring, attach ear wire.

Step 12: Repeat Steps 10 and 11 to complete second earring.

Keys to My Heart Keychain

Make it a little bit easier to tell which keys are yours with this personalized keychain. Stamping a name can also be optional for this project, which makes a great gift for anyone with keys . . . which is everyone!

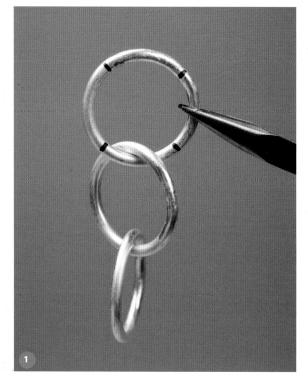

Step 1: Join rings together in a chain.

Step 2: Shape one of the end rings into a square. Using a Sharpie, mark 4 spots that are equidistant from each other **(Figure 1)**. Flatten in between the Sharpie marks using chain-nose pliers, making sure to space the corners of the square equally **(Figure 2)**.

Step 3: Shape the center ring into an oval. To do this, place the tips of your chain-nose pliers inside of the link, centered across from each other. Gently pull the tips of the pliers apart until you get an oval.

Step 4: Shape the last ring into a rounded heart by grabbing a spot on the circle using 2 pairs of chain-nose pliers and bending downward into a V **(Figure 3)**.

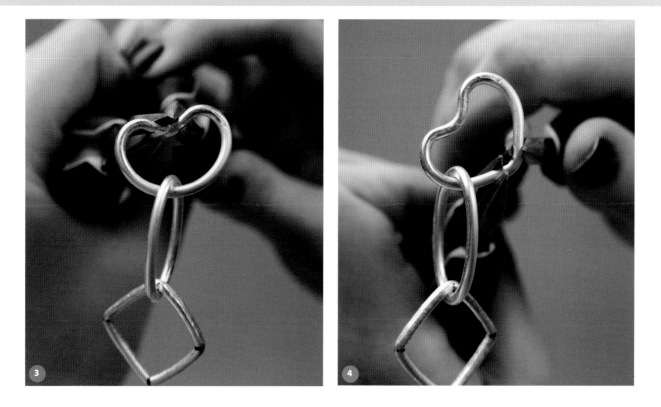

Step 5: Directly across the circle from this V, grab with 2 pairs of pliers and bend another V **(Figure 4)**.

Step 6: Straighten out any waves in the bottom sides of the heart by gently squeezing along the wire with your chain-nose pliers.

Step 7: Using a chasing hammer, hammer all 3 rings flat and texture.

Step 8: Line up stamp on 1 side of the bottom of the heart and, using a household hammer, stamp your name into the ring.

Step 9: Tumble for 30 minutes.

Step 10: Using a Q-tip, apply silver black to the stamped name, taking care not to come into contact with the silver black. Rinse well. Brush lightly over the name with steel wool and polish with a polishing cloth.

Thai One On Component Necklace

Thai silver beads and clasps are made from fine silver, which means they are compatible with fusing! Everybody has a reason to make a statement with their jewelry. Whether you are going to an opening of a show, a party, or just need a really awesome necklace to go with that classic little black dress, this necklace delivers. Use a bold Thai silver pendant to jazz up an already colorful assortment of beads. This necklace is designed to help you use up your last couple of beads left over from a really great project or to showcase a couple of beads you just couldn't live without!

TOOLS AND EQUIPMENT

12 mm, 19 mm mandrels

Wire cutters (I recommend Lindstrom or horse cutters)

Stainless-steel work surface

Firebrick

Butane microtorch

Hot-pliers

Quenching bowl

Bench block

Chasing hammer

Chain-nose pliers

Tumbler and stainless-steel shot

YOU'LL NEED:

Fused rings:
    Small: Three 12mm, 12 gauge
    Large: Four 19mm, 12 gauge

About 36" (91.4 cm) of 22-gauge half-hard sterling silver wire

Thai silver pendant

Four 18mm Venetian glass disc beads: 2 dark aqua with silver foil, 2 peridot with silver foil

Three 15mm Thai silver disc beads

About 6" (15.2 cm) of 5mm sterling silver rolo chain (or enough to get the length you want for your necklace)

1 sterling silver toggle clasp. Pictured: 14mm round toggle clasp with curved bar

Need to Know

Making the cut (page 23)

Fusing a ring (page 26)

Hammering metal (page 27)

Tumbling (page 27)

Basic Chain (page 28)

Wire wrapping a loop (page 118)

Step 1: Using small rings, make a chain of 3 rings.

Step 2: Close and fuse 3 of the large rings.

Step 3: For the fourth jump ring, add a Thai silver pendant and fuse (**Figure 1**).

Step 4: Shape the chain of 3 smaller rings into ovals by placing the tips of a pair of chain-nose pliers into each ring and gently opening them until you achieve an oval. Hammer flat and texture.

Step 5: Hammer flat and texture the ring attached to the Thai silver pendant (**Figure 2**).

Step 6: Two of the large rings should be shaped into octagons. Using chain-nose pliers, make a flat spot on 1 side of the ring by squeezing with the chain-nose pliers (**Figure 3**).

Step 7: Directly across the circle, make another flat spot in the same way (**Figure 4**).

Step 8: In between 2 flat marks, create another flat side with chain-nose pliers (**Figure 5**).

Step 9: Directly across from this flat side, make another flat side (**Figure 6**).

Step 10: In between the flat marks, make 1 more flat side between each to create an octagon (**Figure 7**).

Step 11: For the diamond shape, form a square (see page 86). Put chain-nose pliers in 2 opposite corners of the square. Elongate by pulling the pliers open (**Figure 8**).

Step 12:   Tumble all rings for 30 minutes.

Step 13:   Using sterling silver wire (because it's easier for wire wrapping), form a wire-wrapped loop. Before you close the loop, attach to the center ring (the one with the Thai silver flower).

Step 14:   String 1 glass bead onto the wire and form another wire-wrapped loop. Attach an octagon and wrap the loop.

Step 15:   Attach a wire-wrapped loop to this octagon. String 1 Thai silver bead and join the chain of 3 fused rings.

Step 16:   Wire wrap a glass bead to the fused rings. Attach sterling chain and clasp.

Step 17:   Follow this pattern for side 2, starting from the center ring: 1 Thai silver bead, diamond ring, 1 glass bead, 1 Thai silver bead, 1 octagon ring, 1 glass bead, sterling chain, and clasp.

My Mom's Favorite CZ Earrings

Here's another project using sparkly cubic zirconia beads. They make a gorgeous gift for your mom, but you will be sorely tempted to keep them for yourself. They are floaty and delicate, and you will reach for them again and again for events both fancy and mundane.

TOOLS AND EQUIPMENT

3 mm, 5 mm, 19 mm mandrels

Tronex razor flush wire cutters

Stainless-steel work surface

Firebrick

Butane microtorch

Hot-pliers

Bench block

Chasing hammer

Tumbler and stainless-steel shot

YOU'LL NEED:

Fused rings:

  Small: Four 3mm 22 gauge

  Medium: Four 5mm, 22 gauge

  Large: Two 19mm, 22 gauge; two 19mm, 18 gauge

Twenty 4mm cubic zirconia rondelles, black

1 pair sterling silver ear wires

Need to Know

Making the cut (page 23)

Fusing a ring (page 26)

Hammering metal (page 27)

Tumbling (page 27)

Basic chain (page 28)

Fusing and assembling fine silver (page 30)

Fusing with cubic zirconia beads (page 31)

Attaching an ear wire (page 118)

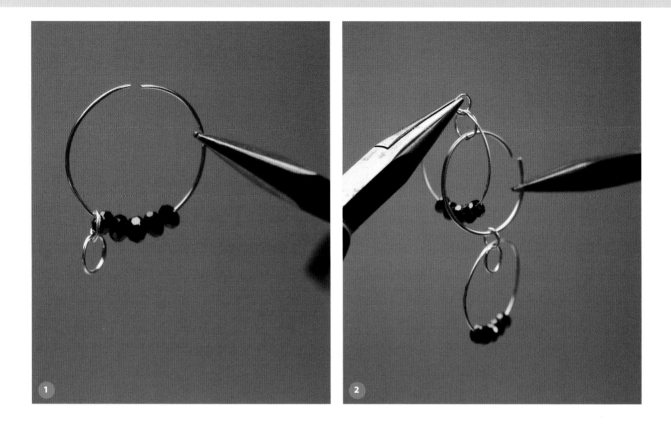

Step 1: Close and fuse all 4 small rings.

Step 2: Attach 1 medium ring to each small ring and fuse.

Step 3: On a 22-gauge large circle, place 5 cubic zirconia rondelles. Pass this ring into a cluster of small/medium rings and fuse, carefully heating the CZs. Repeat 3 times **(Figure 1)**.

Step 4: Using the 18-gauge large ring, link through one 22-gauge large ring and 1 medium ring. Before fusing, join 1 other small ring on this ring **(Figure 2)**. Fuse.

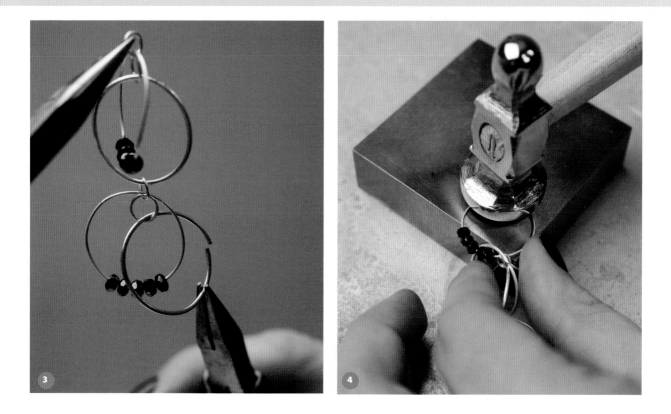

Step 5: On the bottom cluster, link an 18-gauge large jump ring through the 22-gauge large ring and the medium jump ring **(Figure 3)**. Fuse.

Step 6: Repeat Steps 4 and 5 for the second earring.

Step 7: Lightly hammer flat the large rings, being careful not to break the CZ beads **(Figure 4)**.

Step 8: Attach an ear wire to each earring.

Step 9: Tumble for 20 minutes.

Bike Chain Bracelet

Is the man in your life fascinated with your torch? Make him something a bit more butch or make this for yourself for those days when you want something chunky and tough. Wear this and everyone will know you mean business.

Step 1:   Close and fuse all small jump rings.

Step 2:   Link 3 small jump rings on 1 large ring and fuse.

Step 3:   Join 1 large jump ring through the 3 small jump rings from Step 2 and add 3 small jump rings; fuse.

Step 4:   Repeat Step 3 six times.

Step 5:   Join 1 large jump ring; fuse.

Step 6:   Shape all small jump rings into flattened ovals.

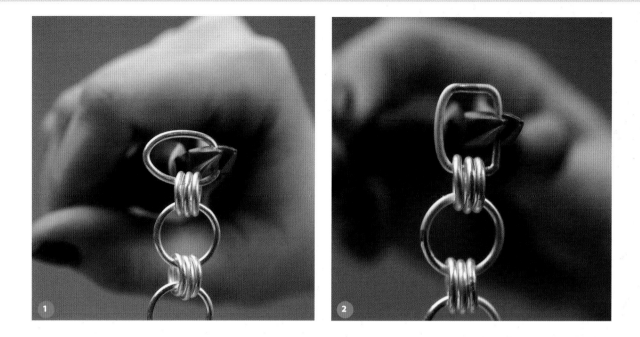

Step 7: Shape all large jump rings into rectangles by pulling large ring into an oval using chain-nose pliers. On the end of each oval, squeeze with chain-nose pliers to flatten. Do the same on other end of the oval to create a rectangle **(Figure 1)**.

Step 8: With chain-nose pliers, flatten along the long sides of the rectangle and then sharpen up the corners **(Figure 2)**.

Step 9: Hammer all large rings flat and texture.

Step 10: Tumble for 30 minutes.

Step 11: Attach a clasp to each end with two 6mm sterling jump rings.

Two-Tone Gold Chain Bracelet

A lot of your fused pieces will prove to be versatile, but this bracelet truly goes with everything. Adding gold-filled chain to your silver fused components turns this into a perfect bracelet to wear every day if you don't like changing up your jewelry with every outfit.

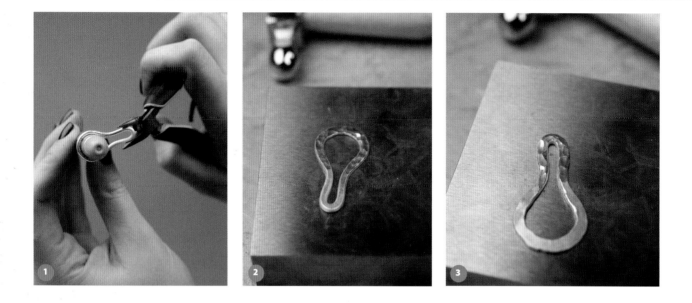

Step 1: Close and fuse all rings (including the large ring you will use for your clasp) separately.

Step 2: Hammer centerpiece and all 3 small rings flat. Texture.

Step 3: Place the Sharpie inside of the large ring for the hook clasp and shape one side of the ring around the Sharpie, closing the other side until there is ⅜" between the sides of the ring **(Figure 1)**.

Step 4: Place the hook part of the clasp flat on the brick. Heat until faintly glowing orange (make sure to stop short of the metal becoming "flowy"!) and quench. This will anneal the metal and make it softer and more pliable for the next step.

Step 5: Hammer the large round part of this clasp flat and texture **(Figure 2)**. Do not hammer the hook side of the clasp yet.

Step 6: Turn the clasp over and hammer the hook part flat; texture **(Figure 3)**.

Step 7: Lay out all of the rings and, using a Sharpie, mark where the holes will go. Holes need to be far enough apart to accommodate your chain. Plan for 6 on the centerpiece (3 on each side), 6 on other links, and 3 on each half of the clasp.

Step 8: Using the smaller bit on the 2-hole punch, punch holes where indicated in each link, including both halves of the clasp.

Step 9: Using chain-nose pliers, bend the hook part of the clasp over until it is just barely open enough to accommodate the other half of the clasp **(Figure 4)**.

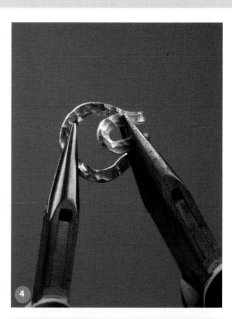

Step 10: Tumble all pieces for 30 minutes.

Step 11: Cut chain to desired length (4 sections, 3 pieces each section). The pieces between the clasp and the first link should all be the same length. The pieces between the centerpiece and the first link should be the same length on the first and third and about 4mm shorter on the centerpiece of chain.

Step 12: Using gold-filled jump rings, join chain to rings to create bracelet **(Figure 5)**.

TIP: While this is a beautiful and secure clasp, the bracelet has to be sized to fit the wrist of the intended wearer. If this bracelet is too loose, the clasp will come unhooked and all of your hard work will be lost on the floor of a movie theater somewhere. It should fit close to the wrist, without being so tight that it limits wrist movement or is uncomfortable.

In Orbit Earrings

Making chain doesn't have to mean that you're limited to necklaces and bracelets. Fusing a few small links together can push an already swinging pair of earrings to the next level. There's a whole lot going on here but because of the fine gauge, the earrings are super-light and surprisingly wearable with even the most conservative of work clothes.

TOOLS AND EQUIPMENT

4 mm, 8 mm, 16 mm, 26 mm mandrels

Tronex razor flush wire cutters

Stainless-steel work surface

Firebrick

Torch

Hot-pliers

Quenching bowl

Chain-nose pliers

Tumbler and stainless-steel shot

YOU'LL NEED:

Fused rings:

   Small: Twenty 4mm, 20 gauge

   Medium: Ten 8mm, 20 gauge

   Medium-large: Two 16mm, 18 gauge

   Large: Two 26mm, 18 gauge

1 pair sterling silver ear wires

Need to Know

   Making the cut (page 23)

   Fusing a ring (page 26)

   Tumbling (page 27)

   Basic chain (page 28)

   Fusing fine gauges (page 30)

   Attaching an ear wire (page 118)

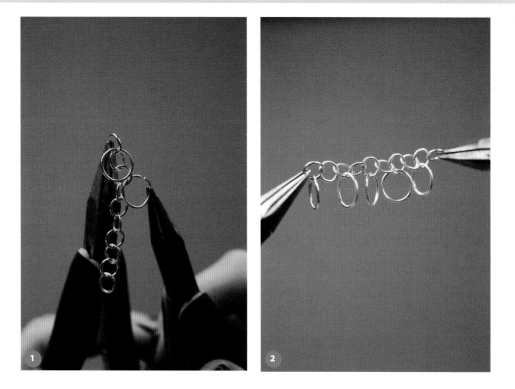

Step 1:   Fuse 2 chains of 10 small links each.

Step 2:   Attach and fuse 1 medium jump ring to the first, third, fifth, seventh, and ninth ring of each chain (**Figures 1 and 2**).

Step 3:   Attach and fuse 1 medium-large ring to the top first link of each chain (**Figure 3**).

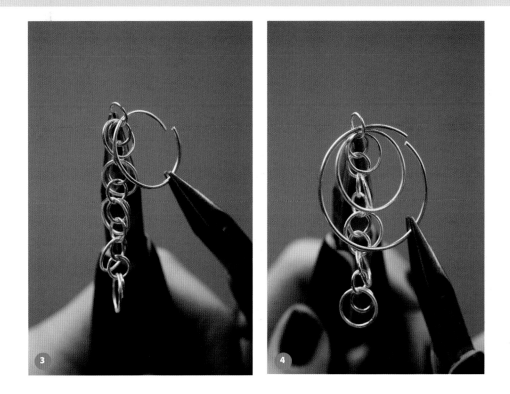

Step 4: Attach and fuse 1 large ring to the same first link of each chain **(Figure 4)**.

Step 5: Attach ear wire to the same first link on each earring.

Step 6: Tumble for 45 minutes.

Going Organic Necklace

Have fun experimenting with different link shapes with this free-form design. It's all silver, which means it will go with everything, but it's also funky enough to stand out. This project will give you the opportunity to bend some wire without worrying about the shape being absolutely perfect. Have fun—the more free-form, the better!

Step 1: Close and fuse 46 small rings.

Step 2: Link 1 large ring through 4 small rings; fuse.

Step 3: Link 1 large ring through 2 of the small rings on this link, add 2 small rings, and fuse large ring.

Step 4: Repeat Step 3 until all closed small rings and all large jump rings are used.

Step 5: Using 1 open small jump ring, link through 2 small rings on end of chain and add clasp **(Figure 1)**.

Step 6: Place chain links in valley so small open ring is flat and carefully fuse. Don't heat up the toggle too much! Make sure to move your torch in a large C shape, not directly heating the toggle **(Figure 2)**.

Step 7: Repeat for other end with other half of clasp.

Step 8: Shape all large jump rings. Randomly grab the wire and pull in different directions using chain-nose pliers. Again, I stress the "random" part.

Step 9: Hammer flat all large jump rings.

Step 10: Tumble for 30 minutes.

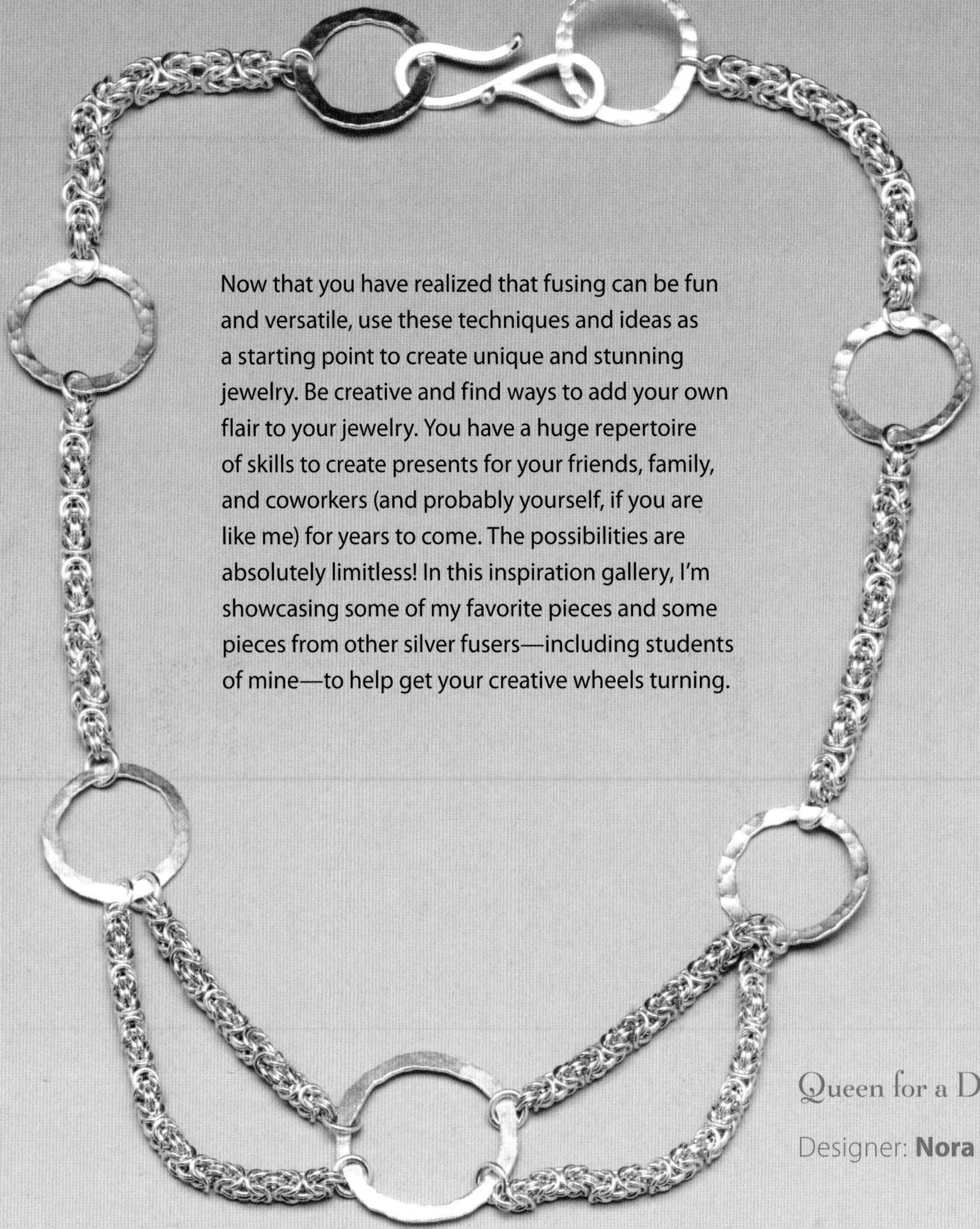

Now that you have realized that fusing can be fun and versatile, use these techniques and ideas as a starting point to create unique and stunning jewelry. Be creative and find ways to add your own flair to your jewelry. You have a huge repertoire of skills to create presents for your friends, family, and coworkers (and probably yourself, if you are like me) for years to come. The possibilities are absolutely limitless! In this inspiration gallery, I'm showcasing some of my favorite pieces and some pieces from other silver fusers—including students of mine—to help get your creative wheels turning.

Queen for a Day Necklace

Designer: **Nora Olsen**

Dreamy CZ Earrings

Designer: **Liz Jones**

Scale It Down Bracelet

Designer: **Nora Olsen**

Mingled Materials Necklace

Designer: **Jennie Stephens**

Life's a Beach Necklace
Designer: **Jennie Stephens**

Green Girl Necklace
Designer: **Liz Jones**

Bob Burkett Necklace
Designer: **Liz Jones**

Rock Candy Necklace
Designer: **Jennie Stephens**

I ❤ Swarovski Necklace
Designer: **Liz Jones**

Loop 'n Loop Necklace
Designer: **Kate Jones**

Charmed Life Necklace
Designer: **Kate Jones**

BASIC TECHNIQUES

WIRE WRAPPING A LOOP

Wrapped loops are a very secure way to turn a piece of wire into a connector for jump rings or other closures. They're a bit difficult to master, but practice makes perfect.

Step 1: Make a 90-degree bend 2" (5 cm) from one end of the wire.

Step 2: Use round-nose pliers to form a simple loop with a tail.

Step 3: Wrap the wire tail tightly down the stem of the wire to create two or three coils. Trim the excess wire.

CRIMPING

Use crimp tubes to secure the end of a beading wire or cord to a clasp or connector. Be patient—this technique takes a little practice, but it ensures a tight closure and professional look every time. Though the projects in this book tell you what length of wire to use, I recommend that you string all of your beads onto the wire before you cut it off of the spool. I find that this saves a lot of wire in the long run.

Step 1: String a crimp tube on the beading wire.

Step 2: Pass through the clasp or connector.

Step 3: Pass back through the crimp tube.

Step 4: Snug the crimp tube close to the closure, leaving enough wire space for the clasp to move around freely. If the wire is pulled too tightly around the clasp, the nylon coating can wear away and eventually break.

Step 5: Spread the two wires so they line each side of the tube, making sure they do not cross in the middle of the tube. Use the first notch on the crimping pliers (round on one jaw, dipped on the other) to squeeze the crimp tube shut, placing one wire on each side of the crimp.

Step 6: Turn the tube onto its side and use the second notch on the crimping pliers (rounded on both jaws) to shape the tube into a tight cylinder. Make gentle squeezes around the tube for perfect rounding.

Step 7: Trim the tail wire close to the tube.

ATTACHING AN EAR WIRE

Clip-ons are findings for nonpierced ears; they have a spring that tightens the metal against the ear. Glue beadwork to the flat portion of the clip, or, if a loop is included, attach the beadwork to the loop at the front of the clip.

French ear wires are J-shaped findings for pierced ears; a loop on one end connects to the beadwork. To use, open the loop as you would a jump ring, add a dangle, and close the loop.

Hoops are wire circles that connect to pierced ears with a finer piece of wire. Slide beads over the wire circle.

Kidney ear wires are pierced-ear findings comprised of a single piece of wire. Connect the beadwork to the dip near the locking portion.

Lever backs have a spring that opens to allow you to put the wire through your ear and closes shut to secure it. Attach beadwork by opening the loop at the bottom of the finding.

Posts are pierced-ear findings made up of a straight piece of wire with a stopper on one end that's secured with an ear nut. Attach earring to the loop below the stopper by opening the loop like a jump ring, adding the dangle, and closing the loop.

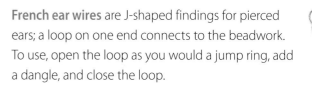

RESOURCES

All of the materials in this book were supplied by Fusion Beads with the exception of the following two items: firebrick (Seattle Pottery Supply) and butane (Calypso Products Inc.).

Alpha Supply
1225 Hollis St.
Bremerton, WA 98310
alpha-supply.com

Beaducation
1347 Laurel St.
San Carlos, CA 94070
(650) 654-7791
beaducation.com

Calypso Products Inc.
PO Box 851075
Richardson, TX
75085-1075
(972) 761-9903
kingbutane.com

Fusion Beads
13024 Stone Ave. N.
Seattle, WA 98133
(888) 781-3559
fusionbeads.com

Jewelry Resource Supply
3601 Greenwood Ave. N.
Seattle, WA 98103
(206) 632-7005
jewelryresourcesupply.com

Seattle Pottery Supply
35 S. Hanford St.
Seattle, WA 98134
(206) 587-0570
seattlepotterysupply.com

INDEX

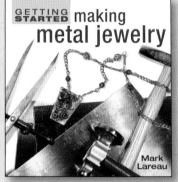
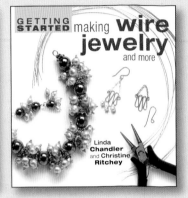